Boondock Kollage

Rochelle Brock and Cynthia Dillard
Executive Editors

Vol. 102

The Black Studies and Critical Thinking series
is part of the Peter Lang Education list.
Every volume is peer reviewed and meets
the highest quality standards for content and production.

PETER LANG
New York • Bern • Frankfurt • Berlin
Brussels • Vienna • Oxford • Warsaw

Regina N. Bradley

Boondock Kollage

Stories from the Hip Hop South

PETER LANG
New York • Bern • Frankfurt • Berlin
Brussels • Vienna • Oxford • Warsaw

Library of Congress Cataloging-in-Publication Data
Names: Bradley, Regina N., author.
Boondock kollage: stories from the hip hop South / Regina N. Bradley
Description: New York Peter Lang, 2017.
Series: Black studies and critical thinking; vol. 102 | ISSN 1947-5985
Identifiers: LCCN 2016056374 | ISBN 978-1-4331-3304-6 (hardcover: alk. paper)
ISBN 978-1-4331-3303-9 (paperback: alk. paper) | ISBN 978-1-4331-4040-2 (ebook pdf)
ISBN 978-1-4331-4041-9 (epub) | ISBN 978-1-4331-4042-6 (mobi)
Classification: LCC PS3602.R34277 A6 2017 | DDC 813/.6—dc23
LC record available at https://lccn.loc.gov/2016056374
DOI: 10.3726/ b10733

Bibliographic information published by **Die Deutsche Nationalbibliothek.**
Die Deutsche Nationalbibliothek lists this publication in the "Deutsche
Nationalbibliografie"; detailed bibliographic data are available
on the Internet at http://dnb.d-nb.de/.

The paper in this book meets the guidelines for permanence and durability
of the Committee on Production Guidelines for Book Longevity
of the Council of Library Resources.

© 2017 Peter Lang Publishing, Inc., New York
29 Broadway, 18th floor, New York, NY 10006
www.peterlang.com

Printed in the United States of America

For Diva Daughter, Ayana Siera
&
For my blood, chosen, and forgotten Kinfolks.
I'm writing myself back to you.

The southern way, no other way, there's no better way to live...
~Field Mob

FOREWORD

In 8th grade, six of us were shipped to this rich white Catholic school called St. Richards after Holy Family, our dilapidated black Catholic school, closed. A few weeks into the year, Ms. Ellington, who tried so hard to make us Holy Family kids feel valued, talked a lot about the work of Eudora Welty, a famous white fiction writer who lived down the street from our school in Jackson, Mississippi.

Ms. Ellington talked a lot about "historical context" when talking about the quirkiness and racism of Welty's characters. I didn't like what "historical context" granted white folks in our English class. If we could understand the weight behind what historical context meant, we could understand how Eudora Welty created fully developed, unreliable white speakers who treated partially developed black objects like "niggers." I felt the weight of "historical context" in that white 8th grade classroom, but I also felt something else I was embarrassed to admit to my friends: I felt a literary tug towards the interior of Welty's stories.

Even though there were massive boundaries between my imagination and Welty's, her opening sentence to the short story "Why I Live at the PO" resonated with me: "I was getting along fine with Mama, Papa-Daddy and Uncle Rondo until my sister Stella-Rondo just separated from her husband and came back home again," I heard something that I wouldn't hear again in a short story for ten years. I didn't just feel a special or familiar relationship to Welty's text and the words; I literally felt special knowing readers who did not and could not call Jackson or Mississippi home loved and really hoped to understand the layers of the familiarity akin to the folks living in Jackson had with one another precisely because of differences in race, class, and gender. I felt and heard Jackson's rumbly human cracks in Welty's work, even though she wrote from a part of Jackson that was very adept at terrorizing and patronizing my people. I knew that we as black folks could do whatever Welty was doing *better* than Welty because our experiences and imaginations were not at all sheltered, cloistered, or white. We could be better because in our present context, future context, and historical context the nation never granted us second chances, healthy choices, or innocence. That, strangely, made us the most human human beings in world.

As a writer, teacher, and reader, I felt nothing like the revelation I got in Welty's stories until I read the first sentence of Toni Cade Bambara's collection, *Gorilla, My Love*: "It does no good to write autobiographical fiction cause the minute the book hits the stand here comes your mama screamin how could you and sighin death where is thy sting and she snatches you up out your bed to grill you about what was going down back there in Brooklyn when she was working three jobs and trying to improve the quality of your life and come to find on page 42 that you were messin around with that nasty boy up the block and breaks into sobs and quite naturally your family strolls in all sleepy-eyed to catch the floor show at 5:00 A.M. but as far as your mama is concerned, it is nineteen-forty-and-something and you ain't too grown to have your ass whipped."

I found Bambara's words after being kicked out of college in Jackson and finding a home at Oberlin College in Ohio. I declared myself an English and Sociology major, and my mentor Professor Calvin Hernton told me that I had no idea what was possible in the short story unless I read the work of Toni Cade Bambara. Bambara took what I most valued in Welty's work and created worlds where no one was sheltered, cloistered, or white. Blackness was historical context in Bambara's short stories and though they were written two and a half decades earlier, I heard not 'just today' in her work. I heard, saw, and felt tomorrow. Toni Cade Bamabara made me want to write fiction.

Twenty years later, I read the sentences "Auntie was skinny and quiet but liked wigs, colored weaves, and high heels. Mama was short and loud, thick-legged, and only liked wearing those tight curls where she sat under the dryer for hours," in Regina Bradley's new book, *Boondock Kollage*. I knew the short story was in the most capable Southern black woman's hands.

As a black boy who has only driven through Albany, Georgia three times and only been to Atlanta twice, Bradley welcomed me into world that is at once lyrically pulsating, unrelenting in its weaving of textured black Southern lessons, and still wholly black and mysterious. *Boondock Kollage* is a southern book. It's a Georgia book. It's an Albany book. It's an Afrofuturist book steeped in black Southern tradition. But it's also a text that takes equal joy in holding the reader's hand, and letting us go. The book trusts and begs readers to follow idiosyncratic characters, ebbs and flows in dialogue, strange scenes that avalanche into the strangest conflicts. *Boondock Kollage* refuses to do the work of native informant literature. It does not shine florescent light on parts of black Georgia, grossly reducing a thumping place into rigid manageable proportions. *Boondock Kollage* is a lot of things, but it is not literary spectacle.

Albert Murray wrote in *The Omni-Americans* that "art is by definition a process of stylization; and what it stylizes is experience." *Boondock Kollage* is not just a wonderfully stylized rumination on the post-Civil Rights South. Like most Southern stories, this book is peopled by black southern characters' foibles and follies but nearly all these characters are aware of what other black characters have to performatively do to survive. In that way, Bradley follows in the tradition of Zora Neale Hurston's *Spunk*. The southern black women characters specifically get a treatment I haven't seen in any contemporary short story collections. They nurture and need nurturing. They trick folks while succumbing to tricksters. They push back against what we now call white supremacist heteropatriarchy while sometimes being willful agents. They are gritty, grimy, pretty, and so damn clean. They are the most essential humans in the communities, with glaring and not so glaring flaws, which makes them most capable of the most incredible magic, majesty, and tragedy.

Regina Bradley has created a comedic tragic oral book that needs to be read by brothers, sisters, mothers, fathers, aunties, grandparents, and their favorite rappers too. The American literary short story needed a reparative black Southern force. Regina Bradley's work is that force and more. *Boondock Kollage* is easily the best and most daring short story collection I've ever read. It made me feel, listen, hear, and ultimately move in ways no other short story collection ever has. Regina Bradley is new at this. Thank God, Regina Bradley feels new at this. But she also feels like she's been here before. We finally have a short story collection worthy of our varied black Southern experiences, and this brilliant, Southern, black book is aptly called *Boondock Kollage: Stories from the Hip Hop South*.

By Kiese Laymon

PROLOGUE

Reckoning

"Gina Lou, we're going into town to get something to eat," my grandfather, who I called Paw Paw, would regularly call out to me in the back of our house on Friday nights. I excitedly climbed into his green Ford pickup truck and watched trees and fields run by my window. We reached the familiar intersection of Hardup and Newton Road and Paw Paw points straight.

"Grandmama grew up down that way," he said. "She ever told you about…"

I've been around storytellers my entire life. I sat on the porches and backyards of numerous folks in my hometown of Albany, GA, listening to folks speak themselves into existence. The best stories were the "cover them ears" stories, the ones about sex or with cussing so the adults shooed us kids into the house or up the stairs to whisper amongst themselves. We had to crane our necks from the top of the stairs or behind the backdoor to catch the joke or hear whom the story was about so we could repeat it to our own friends. My heart jumped at the different types of stories that rendered boisterous laughter; clinking glasses; smacking hands, backs, and bottoms; joyful hollering; grins; and a few silent tears loosened from laughing too hard or remembering strong men and women lost along the journey. In the south, storytelling for black folks is an act of reckoning: stories are memories and memorials, revisions and reclamations, of people's aspirations for the past and future. We are inherent and inherited griots that use stories to conjure, erect, and speak our truths.

My own journey as a storyteller started at my paternal grandparents Nana Boo and Paw Paw's kitchen counter. I sat at the counter eating roasted peanuts or drinking chocolate milk and telling them about what I saw at my pre-school Kid-O-Rama. Sometimes I added to the drama of the story by raising my voice and waving my hands and arms for emphasis (to this day I still talk with my hands). I tested the boundaries of spinning stories and telling stories at their counter, one being hailed as "cute" and the other resulting in the threat of a switch of my own choosing.

After I learned how to write, I continued telling stories, most of the earliest ones being a few sentences long about whether or not I liked the television shows or movies I watched that day, my feelings about the books I borrowed from Southside library – on my own library card of course – and the color of the bows in my hair. Most of the time I used white paper from my grandfather's copy machine and tapped my pencil against my cheeks like the people I saw writing on television. On increasingly frequent occasions, I typed out my handwritten sentences onto the massive grey old-school typewriter paper with runny black ribbon. I loved the sound of the clicking keys. It was slow and methodic, mostly because my small fingers had to locate the right keys and I couldn't type quickly. Typing out my thoughts made me feel important and that what I had to say was equally as important. I would use that typewriter all the way through eighth grade.

I learned quickly via my storytelling and the storytelling of others that the lives of young southern blacks are tethered to the stories of others. Our lives and stories are a reflection of the hopes and expectations of those who came before us. As a member of the post-Civil Rights southern generation, I grapple with the roles that history and collective memory play in articulating my southern black experiences. Black folks' experiences are never solely their own; they are influenced by similar past experiences of the people who share space with them on a daily basis. Being a post-Civil Rights Era black southerner is challenging: how do we find space to speak to our own growing pains and dreams while still keeping present the aspirations and anxieties of the generations before me?

With this question in mind, I mined through my life with a spoon for snatches of conversations, experiences, and images, to bring forth stories that spoke to the jankyness and joys of coming-of-age in the Post-Civil Rights South. The result of my self-reckoning is this collection of short stories titled

Boondock Kollage: Stories from the Hip Hop South. The title is a shout out to hip hop's most underrated rap duo Field Mob, also out of Albany, as well as the notion of patching together different stories to represent the complexities of being young, black, and southern in this contemporary moment. While other historical periods of the American South are well documented, very little attention is focused on the South after the end of the formally organized Civil Rights Movement. The Civil Rights Movement is lodged in mainstream collective memory as the foundation – and the finale – of contemporary southern blackness. The following stories, ranging from spectral to memoir-esque, intend to update how non-southerners and southerners alike think about race and identity in recent memory.

The stories in *Boondock Kollage* present the complexity of contemporary southern black identities often overshadowed in favor of a more recognizable – and easily digested – historicized southern black narrative. *Boondock Kollage* presents the contemporary Black South as a gray space, where past and present cultural touchstones collide and co-exist. The overlap of past and present plays a pivotal role in understanding how southern blackness is constructed.

This collection is divided into three parts. The first section, "Reaching Back Around," consists of four stories about how generational angst and hope is passed down from Jim Crow era (and earlier) generations to post-Civil Rights southern blacks. The second section, "Long Division," consists of five stories that highlight how young southern blacks deal with the aftermath and loose ends of the Civil Rights Movement. The final three stories, a section titled "Stitches in Time," experiments with the question of time and space in the contemporary South.

Finally, I have provided a discussion question bank at the end of the book to explore the issues and themes raised in each story and to help facilitate group discussion. These questions are intended to invite readers to reflect about the renderings of contemporary southern black identities.

ACKNOWLEDGMENTS

I started this project as a dare to myself to rekindle my creative voice. I call her "Gina Mae," the nickname bestowed upon me in Mrs. Adams' eighth grade classroom during my first week of school at Southside Middle School in Albany, GA. I've been courting and trying to get Gina Mae to come out of hiding for almost a decade. She's back and she's got things to say.

Many thanks to Cynthia Dillard for reading an excerpt of a story from my blog and encouraging me to write out loud. Shout out to Kiese Laymon, my mentor and play cousin, for sensing something in my writing that I hadn't felt in a long time. Thank you for advocating on my behalf to write about my country black girl magic. I'd also like to thank my mentors and friends David Ikard, Imani Perry, Mark Anthony Neal, Marcyliena Morgan, Guthrie Ramsey, Lisa B. Thompson, and Sharon Harley for encouraging me to let my southern girl self shine.

I am indebted to the support of the Hutchins Center for African and African American Research at Harvard University and the department of Literature, Languages, and Philosophy at Armstrong State University for making room for me to think and work through my ideas. Specifically, I would like to thank Henry Louis Gates, Krishna Lewis, and Abby Wolfe at Harvard University and Beth Howells, Jane Rago, and Christopher Cartright at Armstrong for their various means of support throughout this process.

XVIII   BOONDOCK KOLLAGE: STORIES FROM THE HIP HOP SOUTH

I am beyond grateful for the opportunity to work with the groundbreakers and game changers John Jennings and Stacey Robinson AKA the dynamic duo Black Kirby. Thank you for taking all of my calls, text messages, instant messages, and smoke signals about the cover for this book and the illustrations for "Some Kind of Wonderful." We're about to change the game with what's coming next. You can put money on that.

A very special thank you to *BOAAT* journal and *Transition* magazine for publishing versions of "A Visitation from Grace" and "Beautiful Ones," respectively.

I have the crunkest sister-circle ever in life! Shout out to my best friend of 20+ years Erica Bridley, my bestie since high school Courtney Holman, and college besties Toni Arnold, Gabrielle Jones, Sheena Burrus Sharper, and Brittany Manson. Much love to my work wifey Bettina Love, the diva feminist Treva Lindsey, the sartorially flawless Tanisha Ford, Emily Lordi, Zandria Robinson AKA Zeezus the Goddess, Brittney Cooper AKA Professor Get Cho Life, the immaculate conjurer Kinitra Brooks, Candice Marie Benbow, Qiana Cutts, Susana Morris, Ashanté Reese, K.T. Ewing, Professional Black Girl Yaba Blay, Rude Gyal Feminist Joan Morgan, Shantrelle P. Lewis, Kaila Story, Aisha Durham, the healer Stephanie Evans, Timothy Anne Burnside, Alisha Lola Jones, Gaye Theresa Johnson, Natanya Duncan, Birgitta Johnson, Jennifer Stoever, Heidi Renée Lewis, Aja Burrell Wood, Aimee Meredith Cox, Dr. Jooksi AKA Fredara Mareva Hadley, the 10th wonder of the world AKA Jessica Marie Johnson, and your favorite editor's favorite editor Liana M. Silva for the countless text messages, bitch fests, hugs, draft reading, and carrying me over the river when I couldn't carry myself. I'd also like to shout out Derrais Carter, Scott Heath, Matthew Davis, Kimberly Bowers, Pete Kunze, David Leonard, Charles McKinney, Brooke Hatfield, Karen Cox, Seneca Vaught, La Marr Jurelle Bruce, Matthew Morrison, and Elliott Powell. I love ya'll. Squad love is the best love.

A thank you and a promise to hug the necks of the following folks for feedback on drafts of this project in its various stages: Josie Pickens, Erica Woods Tucker, Chanda Hsu Prescod-Weinstein, Tawana Jennings, Jamey Hatley, Nicole Terez Dutton, Celeste Ngeve, Robin Boylorn, Darnell Moore, Nikky Finney, Linda Addison, Sheree Renée Thomas, Gholdy Muhammad, Scott Poulson-Bryant, Anquinetta Calhoun, Thaddeus Howze, Carina del Valle Schorske, Natina Adams, Laura Relyea, LaTasha Andrews, Charlie Braxton, Dasan Ahanu, Mecca Jamilah Sullivan, and Rashod Ollison.

Now, I'm from the South. Once I've known you for a few years, I claim you as family. To my friends and brothers of 20+ years, Warren Luke, Jr. and

Clifford Marcus, thank you for such amazing memories and love to inspire some of the stories in this book.

I dedicate this project to the loving memory of Terrell Anthony Warrior, Jason Vaughn, Adrian "AJ" Jenkins III, Roy E. Bradley, Sr., and Jason Williams.

Shout out to my other chosen kinfolks: Doris Cross, Teolar Bradley, Dorothy Woody, Craig Woody, Craig Woody, Jr., Ernestine Lassiter Williams, Patina Bridley, Kyra Lassiter, Roleta Lassiter, LaVeda Thomas, TaShawn Thomas, Roscoe Washington, Amber Chapman, Everett Hayes, Candy Hayes, Barbara Rodolph, Henretta Benson, Woody Givens, Jeanette Givens, Dale Givens, Leslie Harper, Roy Wimbush, Tenia Wimbush, Gloria Anderson, Charity Anderson, Shirley Vaughn, Bobby Vaughn, Melanie Shorter-Jones, Obzeine Shorter, Farris Shorter, Rakia Marcus, Martel Peterson, Kawanis Young, Justin Crenshaw, Jonathon Lawrence, Erika Lawrence, Leland Williams, Nathaniel Williams, Bianca Keaton, Ellis Dumas III, Jervai Dumas, Cameron Beatty, Jeremy Gilmore, Ashley Gilmore, Joseph French, Monique French, LaToya Fields, Terressa Fields, Chelsey Culley Love, Rashaunda Fleming, Yolanda Shipp, Arlesha Coleman, Neadra Cowart, Arkesia Jenkins, Mama Dee Luke, Warren Luke, Sr., John L. Williams, Jr., Brian Dawson, Sr., Cerrice Dawson, Chiquita Safford, Tara Bell, Charles King Jr., Angelica Fowler-King, Archie Fowler, Kanese Rachel, Nina Warrior, Sylvia Wright, Nathan Wright, James Singletary, Quinton Beach, Sr., Vernita Beach, Susie Beach, Velsenna King, Rickie Frazier, Joi Frazier, Eric Francis, Andrea Byrd, Anthony Byrd, Tony C. Jones, Curnesia Bogans, Brittany Ford, Albert Whitehead, Quentin Blanton, Sr., India Blanton, DuCarmel St. Louis, Jenny St. Louis, Marcus Kirlew, Robert Williams, André Mitchell, Elizabeth Mitchell, Derek Arnold, Sam Arnold, Charlotte Arnold, Thelma Odom, Walter Kimbrough, Adria Kimbrough, Tiffany Lee, James Davis, Tauheed Rahim II, Jarvis McInnis, Jerramie Smith, Jermaine Smith, Chester Smith, William Revill, Victor Revill, Leroy Thompson IV, Ontario Wooden, the Dunlap squad: Cheremie, Chelcie, Chenae, Charlene, Mama Patricia, and Daddy Dunlap (R.I.P.), Bradford Gamble, GQ Wallace, Suzy Seay, Sharena "TuTu" Seay, Stephanie Harris-Jolly, Aileen Harris, Melody Addison, Julius Fleming, Julius Bailey, Lanelle Wright Strawder, Arin Harper Wilson, and Cullen Carson. Even if we don't speak every day, there is love. Thank you.

I also want to love on my blood family. Many nights I called on the memory of my Paw Paw, Eugene Barnett, Jr., and my Daddy, Reginald K. Barnett. Thank you to my Nana Boo, Sara Barnett, for those multiple trips to the library in the summers and letting me tell stories even when they got a little too tall. Thank you to my mother, Ilona Stephenson, for celebrating me when I couldn't or didn't know how to celebrate myself. I'd also like to thank my siblings Ebony Washington, Isaiah Washington, and Jeremy Ingram for their endless cheerleading. Much love to my aunties Deidre Ingram and Linda Stephenson and uncles Werner, Don, Norbert, Larry, and Rick Stephenson.

To that guy from Valdosta, my partner-in-crime, my husband, the love of my life, and the great instigator that is Roy E. Bradley, thank you baby. We got here together.

Shout out to Westover High School and the best class of 2002. Shout out to my HBCU, the unsinkable Albany State University and the class of 2006. I'd also like to thank some of the instructors who encouraged me early on to think and write creatively: Ben Bateman, Rebecca Flanigan, Linda Darrah, the late Diane Darby, Stephanie Hankerson, and Joyce Cherry.

Finally, I want to shout out the 'Bany. I did this book for us. Through it all, we survive and strive and love. These are our stories.

TABLE OF CONTENTS

PartThree:
Stitches in Time

PART ONE:
REACHING BACK AROUND

· 1 ·

A VISITATION FROM GRACE

The town of Blackshear was small and shoddy, with small thatch and tar roof houses and one major house made of brick that stood firm on the North shore. Lake Blackshear was the first thing that newly enslaved eyes blinked into focus after their long haul across the ocean. The small ripples wept for them because their eyes were too dry to weep. Blackshear wasn't a "forever" kind of town; it was a brief stop for the beginning of an even longer journey. At the center of Blackshear stood an auction block, a large wooden plank stacked on top of jagged grey and black mismatching stones and rust colored brick. The stones looked like clinched and cracked teeth to complement the tight jaws of the enslaved. One by one, black folks got ate up by winning bids thrown into the world by overly eager and fast talking jaws full of air that acknowledged greedy mouths full of bourbon and no regrets. Black folks got whisked away with white folks' money.

But the auctioneer and the chopping block didn't holler on Sundays, and the enslaved sat on the riverbank restless and waiting. They were careful not to let their eyes fall on one another, in fear of letting compassion grow in their thorny reality. They dug their fingers and toes into the bank waiting for the next auction. Lake Blackshear lapped at their legs, trying to persuade them to look out at the water. Those who pulled themselves together and dared to have enough might looked out at the water and their eyes stopped on a woman who hummed to herself at the farthest bank, past the watchful eyes of white overseers. She was lean and showed no signs of worry. Her joy as she hummed and kicked her feet in the water was seductive and arousing. The small ripples forced themselves to grow into small waves that rushed up her sides with each kick. The woman's humming crept through the water into the ears of those who dared to listen. Nobody knew if she was free by paper or her own will.

Rise Up. Tell them. Tell them to stop choosing us.

The hum beat loud and heavy through the water until one Sunday all the boats rocked in the port. The woman danced and hummed, one foot in the water and the other planted firmly in the sandy brown bank. She didn't sink.

Tell them to stop choosing us.

The enslaved tried to fight it, shaking their heads and shoulders. Hope was a burden. But some black folks hummed and swayed, still not bold or well enough to kick their feet in the water but ready to be free.

As the Sunday woman danced, the lake gurgled and coughed up its bottoms. The water heaved and sucked itself upwards to the wooden limbs of each ship in the port. The water grabbed and snapped the wood while a growing wind shredded its sails. Embarrassed, the ships began to sink. The woman whispered down the front of her blouse into herself. She was named by the black folks "Amazin' Grace" and deemed God's woman. She was the type of Grace black folks needed, not the one the old white man in a robe sung to them about before auction. Grace was a redeemer to some and labeled troublesome by horrified white folks. Blackshear shut down as a slave port after Grace sunk those ships. White folks didn't want to confront no haint of misfortune. They moved further North to Cornflower and Moot Counties, where black folks didn't have a backbone.

But that was way back when.

Shackles fell off and black folks got comfortable.

Now, no one in Blackshear knew much about Grace. Most of the young folks in Blackshear just shrugged her off.

"She's just some old lady," they said.

Grace lived on the banks of Lake Blackshear in a house never wind whipped or eroded by the water. Blackshear elders said she stood out on the bank every morning communing with the dead. Grace couldn't kick her feet in the water anymore without pain, but she made herself available to the whispers. She knew better than the young folks that morning was for the ancestors. They would sweep through the town as a soft mist, curious about the newer world and if they still had a place in it. After their journey, the ancestors collected at Grace's feet as she stood on the shore, hugged her legs, and seeped back into the lake to rest. But some wistful mornings, Grace knew they were agitated, nipping at her heels and demanding extra attention. It was hard work to follow their beckoning. Her body wanted to pass the fight on to someone with younger bone marrow and redder blood, but in the quietest corner of Grace's spirit she knew she still had work to do. Her work weighed on her joints and bones more than time itself.

On those anxious mornings, Grace then hobbled through the leftover mist into the middle of town now called called Gomorrah Square. A man named Mr. Earnest met her at the old auction block. Mr. Earnest was the color of ripe corn silk. He was Grace's fetcher and looked considerably younger than Grace but stretched his shoulders apart to make him fill up more of the world. Mr. Earnest lifted her up past the first step and kept a steady gaze on her to make sure she didn't fall as she made her way to the top of the platform.

Grace huffed and climbed each rickety stair to the top of the wooden platform and steadied herself on the worn podium. Mr. Earnest moved to the right side of Grace at the bottom of the block. Only Grace touched the dented and rusting black box under her arm. Flecks of red jumped from each scratch and dent. Folks called it the speakerbox. With each turn of the crank the veins in Grace's hand pop through her papery thin skin. The speakerbox never spoke on the first crank. But on the third turn, it cackled and wheezed to life. A faint sound of a man's voice pushes through the static. The man's voice, a quiet vibrato, snakes through the square and around Blackshear.

"Freddie's dead." The sounds of guitars and violin strings wrap around the town. A flute as sweet as a chirping bird breaks free through the cackling and pops of noise.

"That's what I said."

Morning gatherings were nicknamed "early service" because the ground was still wet and the dew tried to settle itself in between blades of grass to avoid the sun. People stirred from their houses and headed to Gomorrah Square. Early service was attended by the same families: the Davises who ran the market; the Teaks, who were the oldest family in Blackshear; the Bluffs, the less-than-respectable family that owned the local juke joint; the Grays, who worked in the church; and the Crisps, who worked the Teaks' farming land in the northern part of the county.

"Freddie's dead," the voice echoes.

The strings and trilling flute agree with the singing man.

Grace stands tall as age will allow her. The speakerbox shuts off and Grace speaks to the crowd.

"Freddie was chosen," she says in a scratchy voice. The townspeople stand silently and shuffle in place. "We'll stop choosing them when they stop choosing us." Menfolk fretfully rub their chins. Faint sounds of bristling stubble sit in the air. Womenfolk clutch their chests and sway in place. Nobody looks for Freddie's parents.

After Grace's announcement, folks slump off to their houses. It was time to prepare for Freddie's benediction. They sift through their cupboards to find something to cook and share with Freddie's parents. "Such a shame," Mrs. Gray says as she fights a sticky dough ball to make buttermilk biscuits and a crust for pecan pie. "This is the second time we're showing up to Ava and Beam's house this year." Ava and Beam Lay had two girls and four boys. Their oldest boy Ant was chosen at the beginning of the year. Now Freddie, their third boy, was chosen in the late Spring. Mr. Gray shakes his head and rattles his newspaper.

"A house full of black boys and black girls ain't safe in this world."

"Tell the truth," Mrs. Gray sighs. She works the dough a little harder saying "mmph," between each punch.

When people arrive at the Lay house the front door is cracked open. Beam sits blank-faced in the corner of his living room, his arms outstretched towards his wife, who is pacing the opposite side of the room. Ava lets people guide her to a chair next to her husband but she says little. The visitors pat the hands and heads of Ava, Beam, and Freddie's baby sister Tater. Tater twists and stretches her legs out to get on the floor and out of her mother's iron grip. The Lays' other children, along with Freddie's cousin Almond, sit in their rooms away from the adults. Ava tries to pull away from each touch.

"I ain't got nothing left to choose," Ava sobs. Beam hides his face between his hands. His wife stomps her feet and throws her hands in the air. "You hear me?" she screams. "Nothing left!" The women gently touch each other's sides and try to pull Ava back into her chair. The stricken woman calls out for her dead boy. "You can come back to us," she whispers. "You don't have to stay bright. Nothing calls for something as tender as you, Freddie." Ava claws at her face. Thin lines of blood run down her cheeks. "I can be chose for you," Ava nods and reaches into the air. "See baby? Here." She pats her lap. "Come on, now. Switch places with Mama."

"She's out of her head with grief, Lord, and there's nothing we can do," the women whisper into each other's ears and necks. The benediction for being chosen is not new. It is tradition.

***

Mayfield lived in Grace's basement. Even though he graduated on time, most folks in Blackshear thought he was dull. He seldom said a word out loud. Mayfield hated to talk because his words and thoughts never matched up quite right. They thought he was like his Mama, Fancy, an awkward girl with a droopy sandy brown half-fro that haloed around her head. Fancy was a distance cousin of the Bluffs on her Daddy's side. Nobody knew who could be Mayfield's Daddy, but the women didn't push it past any of the men because even a girl who lived in her head could catch a wayward and lustful glance. Fancy said she saw red and purple and yellow fairies fall from the sky and dance on the Lake after dark. As a baby, Mayfield looked strewn across Fancy's body, sliding across her chest and hips in a loose baby sling as Fancy skipped up and down the roads, pointing at the stars and the lake while cooing to the top of Mayfield's head. "See, baby boy? They creep across the water like you crept up in my womb." She would click her tongue against her teeth and hoist Mayfield back up her side as he slipped towards her legs. Fancy fed Mayfield powdered sugar and milk for breakfast. "Star creepers eat star dust," she said. Mayfield would laugh and clap his fat baby hands into the sweet mixture and dunk his sticky hands into his mouth.

When Mayfield could walk, he stumbled alongside his long-stepped Mama and then fell strides behind her. She'd wait for him on the shore and pat the water with her hands, trying to get her fairies to dance. "It's okay. It's okay," she'd sing. "I have him with me."

One night, Fancy sat Mayfield on the porch of their next door neighbor Mrs. Flint. She was a widow and all her children were grown and scattered across the state. Mrs. Flint liked Fancy and loved Mayfield, giving him small peppermints out of her purse and an ever-ready hug around his growing middle. Fancy jumped off the last step to take Mayfield's cheeks into her hands.

"Mrs. Flint gone take care of you now, my little star creeper," she said. Mayfield struggled to find the words "no. Stay." Instead he blinked and reached for her with watery eyes. Fancy gently lowered his arms and pointed upward. "They said my time here is done. They're back talking to me. Time. Time. Time." She made a funny face to get Mayfield to smile. With a turned back Fancy said, "You are your own hope, son" and skipped out of Mrs. Flint's yard to the left towards the lake. Mayfield couldn't get his words and voice to work together to get Fancy to stay. She disappeared into the dusk with a small cloud of dust behind her. It was then and there on Mrs. Flint's doorstep that Mayfield slipped further into himself, hoping to scrape together pieces of love from the final lingering smell of his mother or any other secret places she may have stayed in his brain.

Mrs. Flint found him on her porch and looked out into the road, swishing her head left to right like she was crossing the street. "Lord, Lord," she said. Mayfield clicked his teeth like his mother, trying to hold on to her memory.

Mrs. Flint treated Mayfield like her own blood, sending him to Sunday School and attending all of his parent-teacher conferences. Mayfield tried to do right by Mrs. Flint, who insisted he learned to love her by referring to herself as his "Auntie Gertie," by sweeping the porch and mowing the front lawn. She never pushed him to talk, instead rocking in her favorite chair listening to the radio or watching the news. Sometimes Mayfield sat at her feet and laid his head in her lap for her to scratch it.

When Mrs. Flint died she didn't show any sign of sickness. She just stopped breathing right in the heat of August and before the start of Mayfield's senior year. Even though people stopped by to pay their respects, they whispered about what would happen to Mayfield. Nobody wanted to take the mute boy in. Not even Mrs. Flint's grown children, who Mayfield thought of as his kin. But Grace and Mrs. Flint were friends and she took it upon herself to move the boy in with her. "You ain't got to stay here by your lonesome," she said. "You got a place with me if you want it."

The next week, a beat up small leather suitcase with a stubborn zipper in hand, Mayfield knocked on the lake house door. He'd only seen Grace with Mrs. Flint a couple of times, but the two women together seemed happy when they visited. A breeze from the water kissed his cheek. He thought he heard someone humming. Mayfield craned his neck towards the water. The shore was empty but the hum washed in and out with each wave.

Star creeper.

Grace opened the door. She looked the boy over once and rubbed her hand down his arm. "You can hear me okay, can't you boy?" Mayfield nodded and shrugged his heavy shoulders. "I set you up downstairs," she said, moving aside to let the boy come inside. The smell of roasting corn, potatoes, and fried cubed steak sneak out of the kitchen. Mayfield's stomach rumbled and Grace smiled. "Gertie told me before that it's your favorite meal," she said. "Gone and put your stuff downstairs and wash up to eat." Mayfield bent over to hug the old woman. It doesn't feel natural but necessary. Grace patted his back with one open hand like a light church hug. "Alright now," she grunted through his shoulder. "Alright." The boy's flip flops slapped against the floor. "You can stay long as you can stand it," she said to his slumped back. "Just respect my house and always answer when I call you, hear?" Mayfield continued shuffling his feet in and out of his flip flops against the aging hardwood floors. They groaned under his weight.

In the basement, Mayfield stretched out on the brown and yellowing sofa bed careful not to knock over the skinny floor lamp and desk next to his bed. A grey bubble screen television sat unused in the corner. Mayfield stared up at the ceiling and then out the window into the lake. He thumped his throat with his forefinger and thumb. An itch climbed above his Adam's apple into the back of his throat. It flared up like an allergy and Mayfield clicked the back of his throat with his tongue to soothe himself.

Mayfield never went to Gomorrah Square for early service because he heard the speakerbox from the basement. He pushed his fingers through the white venetian blinds to see who came to the square for the news. As usual, he saw Mr. Earnest reach out to grab Grace by the hand and forearm. After the announcement, Mayfield watched people stumble home. Grace pointed towards the house. Mr. Earnest nodded. They stop on the front porch and talk in muffled voices.

"Are you sure bout this one?"

"Chose is chose," Grace said and the screen door slammed shut behind her. Grace called down into the basement with the might of God.

"Mayfield, be ready to go with Mr. Earnest this evening," she said. Something popped in Mayfield's chest. He thumped his throat.

"You hear me? Mr. Earnest'll come fetch you this evening." Grace closed the door.

The day pulled the sun down faster than usual, like it refused to witness what was about to take place. In the basement, Mayfield's lamp cast flickered light across the basement. The shadows against Mayfield's body gave him wings. Chirping crickets and lolling waves filled the air. Mayfield ignored the rapping at the basement door. Unanswered knocks grew into angry thwacking. Mayfield ignored the knocking again. The door cracks under Mr. Earnest's heavy hands and Mayfield jumps up. He hits his head on a shelf. He grunts and blinks hard to focus his sight. Heavy boots clump down the stairs. Mayfield sees Mr. Earnest in overalls and a brown leather brimmed cap. He stands like a man who was once a terror. Mr. Earnest towers over Mayfield's slouch.

"Time to go, boy," Mr. Earnest says. "Don't make me move furniture to get you out of here."

Mayfield unwillingly releases a sigh.

"I tried to put in a good word for you, son." Mayfield shakes his head no.

You are your own hope.

Mayfield doesn't break eye contact with Mr. Earnest. He moves behind his unmade sofa bed.

My little star creeper.

"Don't make this harder than it is," Mr. Earnest says. "You a biggun. And I'm getting old."

Mayfield flicks a bird. Mr. Earnest's face scrunches up and he clinches his fists.

Mayfield bends over and looks for something to throw. He grabs the brick that steadies the sofa bed. Mayfield raises the brick and his arm like a quarterback. Grace hollers from the top of the basement stairs.

"Mayfield! When I call you answer, boy! Mr. Earnest is doing this for me!"

Mayfield lowers the brick but grips it in his hand until his knuckles turn white.

"When I call you answer! That was the deal."

Another whimper escapes Mayfield's scratchy throat.

"You got chose, boy." Mr. Earnest inches closer to Mayfield. Mayfield drops the brick.

"Chose is chose." Mayfield crumples onto the bed into a heap of sobs. Mr. Earnest hoists him up by his black shirt and out of his flip flops. Grace meets them at the stairs. Mayfield fixes his gaze on the ground.

"Day is gone," Grace said. "We ain't alone." She looks out at the lake and whispers down into her shirt. "Tell them to stop choosing us." The water in the lake roars. Specks of light dance across the top of the water. Grace puts her hand on the top of Mayfield's head.

"I know you don't understand," she says. "but nothing ain't never free. It's hard and unhealthy where we starting from," she sighs. "I thought I paid the price for us. I tried to choose myself way back when. I wanted to just end it. All of the foolishness." Grace puts her hand under Mayfield's chin to lift his face. "But it weren't enough. Weren't ever enough." Mayfield sees the specks of light dance on the tips of his eyelashes.

Mr. Earnest lugs Mayfield's defeated body to the bed of his pickup. He drives slowly under the moonlight, each tree branch catching a ray and passing it along Mayfield's body. Gomorrah Square is quiet and misty. They are not alone. A white van with open back doors flashes its lights from the front of the auction block. Two men stand on either side of the van.

"He got chose?" One of the uniformed men reached out to take Mayfield's arm. Mayfield doesn't look up from the ground.

"Yep." The men nod and throw Mayfield into the back of the van. The sound of slamming doors startles tears from Mayfield's eyes. There was no love left to be scraped.

No one in Blackshear knew much about Grace, the old black woman who lived on the banks of Lake Blackshear in a house never wind whipped or eroded by water. Every morning, Grace stood on the banks, ankle deep in the spirits of ancestors. It was time for another benediction. Grace hobbled to Gomorrah Square with Mr. Earnest at her side and huffed up the steps to the top of the wooden platform. She cranks the speakerbox. On the third crank a gentle vibrato of a man's voice snaked through the square against flutes, guitars, and violin strings.

"Mayfield's dead," the voice crackles. "That's what I said."

· 2 ·

INTENTIONS

Albany, Georgia's Dream Week started in the 1980s as a way to say "thank you" to the men and women who protested on Albany's behalf during the Civil Rights Movement. Folks wanted to be remembered past Black History Month and, like pretty much everyone else, wanted to have a piece of Dr. King's legacy. One year, his daughter came on behalf of the King family to the legacy banquet. She didn't make the front page of the paper but a small picture of Ms. King was on page 3E of the "About Town" section.

Dream Week always happened after Spring Break. All school age kids submitted a project that was appropriate for their grade level. This would be my twelfth Dream project. As a second grader, I wrote a poem "What Civil Rights Means to Me? Thank You." My teacher and classmates applauded because I made the last two lines rhyme: "Thank you Dr. King. You're the reason we are still in this thing." In seventh grade, I submitted a shadow box of Laurie Pritchett throwing people in jail. Laurie Pritchett was the Chief of Police in Albany during the movement. My great aunt Mabel didn't seem to mind him.

"He wasn't rude and directly racist like them other white folks 'round here," she said. My great Uncle Clyde, however, didn't agree. As soon as Aunt Mabel finished her sentence he was quick to add, "just because he wasn't *openly* a cracker doesn't mean he wasn't a cracker."

Other family members offered their suggestions to make my project more realistic. "Make that guy look more like me. I was there," my Uncle Junie laughs and points at the brown stick figure with a fistful of black painted cotton balls as a head. "I had more hair back then. Put more black cotton balls on that dome!" His wife, Auntie Rene, sucked her teeth. Nobody could tell for sure when Uncle Junie was telling the truth or spinning a story. He always thought everything was about him. "You been bald since '61, man," Auntie Rene laughs. Uncle Junie leaves me be to finish my project.

My freshman year of high school I interviewed Sadie Harris Johnson, a painter who attended my church. She didn't march but told me she was the best sign maker in southwest Georgia. "I couldn't be denied in my effort for that," she said. "My protest was bold letters and bright construction paper." She let me take pictures of some of her most well known signs and display them on PowerPoint for my presentation. I got an A- because my teacher took off points for fuzzy picture edges and a few grammar errors.

For my final dream project, I was stuck. I was already suffering from senior-itis – I didn't want to do a damn thing but walk across the stage and gradu-ate in May. My history and homeroom teacher Mr. Bayman expected us to submit a report or creative project highlighting an event or significant person in the local movement. For the most part, Bayman was cool – especially if you brought him a fried egg and chicken biscuit from Pearly's Kitchen. "Fried egg and chicken biscuits won't save me from failing you," he warned. "No Dream project? No graduation."

At first, I thought about mapping out Dr. King's marching routes and church sermons in Albany. I wanted to call it "Ain't No Half-Stepping to Freedom: King's March though the Good Life City," but I didn't feel like going to Central Library to research the old newspapers and plot out King's path. Besides, I hated dealing with the old drunk man that posted up on the corner and smelled like piss. He talked to himself as he stumbled down the street.

This year's Dream Week started on the Saturday of Spring Break with Beatitudes Missionary Baptist Church's "Keep the Dream Moving: a Day of Service." I told my Mama I'd skip community service to go work on my proj-ect.

"When is the project due, son?"

"Monday."

"As in three days from now?"

"Yes, ma'am." Mama shook her head. "Have you started on it at all?"

"I've been playing with a few ideas. I got it taken care of."

Mama looks up and stares like she wants to burn a hole in the middle of my forehead. I've been a foot taller than Mama for two years now but she makes sure I don't forget she could whoop me. Mama's got heavy hands. "Make sure you got this project taken care of, Dap." She pokes a finger into my chest. "If you don't turn in that project, please believe you will get these hands on you and I'm not a preacher. There won't be enough Balm in Gilead to heal you if you don't graduate, hear?"

"I got it, Mama."

She pokes me again with two fingers. "Oh. And you are going to do that community service tomorrow. I promised your Auntie Delia you'd be a server in the soup line this year."

I groan. Mama pushes her index finger to her lips. "But I'd be at the church all day! The library closes at five on Saturdays." Mama crosses her arms across her chest.

"Be ready to go at 9 A.M. sharp. Ain't nobody told you to wait until the last minute."

***

Beatitudes Missionary Baptist Church converted their gym into a soup kitchen on Mondays, Thursdays, and Saturdays. Dream Week brought an overflow of volunteers to the church. Even though I can drive, Mama insists on driving me. Auntie Delia waves from the gym entrance. Mama and Auntie Delia have been friends since they were three years old. They lived next door to one another and were opposites in everything: Auntie was skinny and quiet but liked wigs, colored weaves, and high heels. Mama was short and loud, thick-legged, and only liked wearing those tight curls where she sat under the dryer for hours. I've never seen Mama in anything yellow or pink like Auntie. She waves Auntie Delia to her side of the car. After they kiss each other on the cheek, Mama says "Put him on the front lines, Dee." Auntie laughs and winks. A bright blue curl gets caught on her eyelashes. "Gone and get out the car, nephew. Put on some gloves and the server's net I left for you on the front table."

I shrug and look around the gym. My god brothers, Dawson and Fleet, are setting up tables. Dawson is six months older than me but we're in the same class. Fleet is a junior. I nod at Fleet. He starts to nod but his head stops midway in the air. Fleet points at my head and laughs. "What the hell is that on your head?" he mouths. He nudges Dawson and points at my head. They both laugh. I point at them and then smack the front of my pants. Someone clears their throat behind me.

"Your ladle, sir," Auntie Delia slightly bows and presents me with a serving spoon.

"Just like Jesus." She pinches and twists my shoulder. Nobody loves Jesus more than my Mama and Auntie Delia.

"Watch your mouth, boy. That name is too good for your foolishness."

Folks start coming into the gym around 11:00AM. Pastor Barner stands at the door shaking hands, slapping people's backs in encouragement, and hugging the children wrapped around his legs. Folks are thankful that Deacon Willer doesn't say grace because the food won't get cold. Auntie Delia marches to the front of the tables and taps on the microphone sitting on a projector stand.

"Okay folks, good morning! We want to get you fed as quickly as possible. Amen?" People nod and applaud. Auntie Delia smiles. "We'll line you up by tables. Please do not line up until your table is called." After their table is called, people drag themselves to the back of the gym to eat. Jiffy cornbread, chicken noodle soup, turkey sandwiches, and chips are at each station. I ladle soup into the eager hands holding fading white cups and bowls. Adults silently nod and shuffle to the next station. They do not look servers directly in the eye. The sounds of squeaking sneakers, rustling jackets, and loose-soled shoes fill the gym. Young kids stand on their tiptoes to look over the counter. They tug at holey shirts and point to a sandwich or bag of chips.

"That one!" a head full of pigtails pipes up from underneath the counter. A little brown finger points at the front sandwich wedge. Down the line, another little hand grabs at two potato chip bags. I lean over the table to see the hands' owner.

"Gimme!" A little boy in a dingy white baseball hat yells at me as he stomps his foot. The boy's mouth is pulled like he's sucking on a Sweet and Sour tart. The man he is with shakes his head in apology and grabs the boy's arm.

"Don't be greedy son," the man whispers. The boy isn't satisfied. He kicks his shoe into the floor and bounces his head up quickly like he has a brilliant idea. "Can I have it if I eat aaaall my foods Daddy?" the hat swallows the back of the boy's neck as he looks up to his father waiting for an answer.

"We'll see." Auntie Delia kneels and smiles at the little boy. He runs behind his dad's leg.

"You been a good boy for some extra chips, baby?" The boy buries his face into his dad's worn jeans. Auntie Delia looks up to the man. "How old is he?" she asks. The man chuckles and shakes his head. "Just turned four last month." Auntie Delia lays her hand on her chest and sighs. "I got two boys myself. Eighteen and sixteen." She points at Dawson and Fleet, who are trying to hang a welcome sign at the front door. "I miss 'em at this age. His little days will go by fast." The man turns to leave, gently dragging his son behind him. Auntie Delia stuffs the extra bag of chips into the man's coat pocket.

I catch myself smiling.

***

After Auntie Delia gives us the okay, I sit with Fleet, Dawson, and their cousin Bam on the picnic table for lunch in the back churchyard. Bam is a freshman. On most days of the week, Bam wore his favorite shirt, a raggedy orange hoodie with a big "A" on the front pocket. His voice sounded like he wasn't sure if he was ready to be a man. Between bites of a turkey sandwich stuffed with BBQ chips, Bam fumbles around in his front pocket and pulls out a fading box of cards. Dawson stomps his feet on the grass.

"Aaaaaaaye. You really want this whoopin' in front of the Lord, boy?" Bam sucks his teeth and shakes the cards out of the box like a pack of cigarettes. The jokers are bent at the corners and a red star is marked on a card with the card company name. It's the little joker.

"I hate when you shuffle Bam," Fleet groans. "You always give me stupid cards."

"You just can't play, baby brother," Dawson laughs.

"Whatever." Fleet sucks his teeth in disagreement. "How can you win with a hand full of hearts? That nigga just can't shuffle."

"We playing joker-joker deuce-deuce right?" Bam shifts through the deck to pull out the deuce of hearts.

"Bam deal the cards right this time. I mean it!" Fleet playfully shoves Bam's shoulder. "Not like last time when you dealt yourself two at a time."

"The cards were sticking, cuzzo," he said.

"Uh huh." Fleet twists his mouth and points to it. "Ole cheatin' ass boy."

I look back towards the church. The kitchen backdoor is open. Laughter and Tye Tribbett creep out the open door. Gnats swarm in the warm air coming from the hole in the screen mesh. Dawson waves his hand in my face to bring me back to the table.

"Stop looking for my mama," he whispers. "That'll make her show up."

"You know your mama's like the CIA," I laugh. "She's a silent killer."

Fleet doesn't respond because his face is deep in his hand. His scrunched brows say Bam did him dirty on the cards again.

"I told you Bam can't deal." He glares to his left at Bam. "I got two and a possible," Fleet sighs. "You got us big brother?" Dawson smirks. "We gone be aight. Five and a possible."

I curve my cards in so Dawson can't see that I got both jokers.

"Quit lying Boonk!" Boonk went to school with us and lied about everything. Everybody but Dawson laughs. "I ain't no Boonk! I don't lie about the color of my shirt!" We laugh again. "You ain't running nothing, sir," I say. "I got that work in these cards!" I look at Fleet and shrug. "Bam dealt me right."

A high pitched voice creeps up behind us. "Ya'll ain't nothing but some heathens. Playing cards at church." Dawson jumps, afraid it's his Mama. Bam's little sister, Tilly, laughs. Tilly used to run behind us and cry if she didn't get her way. She turned thirteen last month and started wearing a training bra her Mama bought her from Forever21 and now she thinks she's grown. Bam clutches his chest and feigns offense. "No. No, Tilly Mae! I am playing cards outside on this raggedy picnic table in God's good air."

Tilly shakes her head and walks towards the kitchen. "Still a heathen." Bam snaps Tilly's bra strap with his free hand. "I'm your sister. That's nasty." She punches him. "All it is a training strap. It's just holding up that big head of yours. Ain't nothing there." Bam pats his chest.

We laugh.

Tilly stomps off to the kitchen. We turn back to our game and I start to think about Monday's deadline.

"Aye, D, did you finish that assignment for Bayman's class?"

Slam. Scrape.

"Yeah I got most of it, man," Dawson nods his head. "I whipped up something on my Uncle Andrew King."

"Yeah? Ya'll related to Martin Luther King?"

Dawson shakes his head. "Ionno. But he was bragging bout escorting Martin Luther King around Albany."

"Don't forget the 'the,'" Bam says.

"What?" Fleet laughs.

"The 'the,' you uneducated negro. Martin Luther 'THE' King. Be respectful." Bam shuffles his hand

Scrape. Scrape.

"Anyway." Dawson scoops the book up with his card. "Unc Andrew talked about how folks came out to hear Martin Luther THE King " – Dawson rolls his eyes at Bam –"speak. You know them churches on Whitney Avenue? He said Dr. the King walked across Whitney Avenue to talk to two packed church houses at the same time."

He got a real good project.

"Yeah," Dawson continues. "Unc said he would've been arrested too but he had to get up early for work the next day."

"Sounds like Unc punked out."

Dawson shrugs.

"Would you go to jail willingly, Dap?"

"Hell naw. You know my Mama, right?"

Slam!

My card spins in the middle of the table.

"Auntie still trippin' on you huh?"

"Man. Is she graduating or me?"

"She's probably saying 'OUR diploma' like my Mama AKA your Auntie Delia."

More laughter.

"What you got for your project so far, Dap?"

"Not a damn thing."

"Ain't a fried egg and chicken biscuit big enough in the world to save you from failing if you don't turn in that project."

I reach across the table and shake his wrists. Dawson's hands clamp down on the cards.

"Stop fool!"

I twist my mouth in thought and look out into the small grove of pecan trees across the street.

"I'm so ready to get up outta here man."

"Albany ain't so bad, folk." "Albany is the trap. We stuck."

"On?"

"Everything. Like this damn Dream Week." I curl my fingers into air quotes. "We act like MLK is buried over in the fancy white people cemetery on Dawson Road." Crown Hill cemetery had regular burials where people could be buried underground or in big marble mausoleums above ground.

"Not the white people graveyard though." Dawson cackles. Bam and Fleet fake sing "Going Up Yonder."

"I mean, why do we do this shit every year? I get it. Be thankful."

"Say that!" Fleet waves his hand like the old women who sit in the front pews at church.

"They want you to go up yonder, Dap." Fleet points his bony index finger upward.

He hops on the tabletop, his arms spread wide and above his head. Fleet's eyes are squeezed shut until his eyelids wrinkle. He puffs out his cheeks.

"You look constipated, Fleet." He ignores me.

"Won't He do it?!" He hums loudly and shakes his hands over my head. "Good lord if you hear me, your humble servant, PLEASE let this young and dumb black boy graduate on time." Dawson and Bam fan themselves and say "On time! Glow-ray."

"We need this miracle today, Jesus."

"TODAY LAWD!"

"Ya'll ain't – "

The table violently shifts to the left. Fleet falls and kicks Bam in the face. "SHIT!"

A man in a wrinkled dookie brown suit and yellowing shirt looks past us towards the parking lot. Bam rubs his jaw.

"You good? My bad, cuz." Bam waves Fleet's hand away. "Yeah I'm good." Fleet turns to the man to say something. "Sir?" The man keeps walking away from us. Fleet yells into the man's back. "Aye mister! That was one hell of an apology! Thanks so much!" Fleet stretches out his legs and flops to the side of the table and points at Bam. "You made me kick my cousin!"

The man brings his gaze back to us. His eyes are dull like the copper sponges on Mama's kitchen sink that have soaked up too much greasy water and scrubbed too many pans.

"Shutup you little shit!" Dookie Brown yells. "Watch where you sitting at the table next time."

Dawson gets up to defend his brother.

"Don't get got old man."

The man's neck rolls in small circles like the females at school as he talks.

"Sit down somewhere, boy Dawson." Dawson's fists loosen and he squints at the man to try and place him. "I know your mama working over there in that kitchen." The man's neck continues to roll. He turns to me.

"What about you, boy? You got something to say?" He burps in my face. Dookie Brown kicks the other legs of the picnic table.

"Ya'll do this every year and serve the same shit. Store brand soda and sandwiches made with the Dollar General turkey and government cheese."

"We don't have to make your ungrateful ass a damn thing," Fleet mumbles to himself.

"I come because ya'll owe me. You little niggers running round here like you run the goddamn city and don't know how to pee straight." We all flinch. Bam stares the man down. But something pushes through Dookie Brown's glare that softens Bam's back. He forces his head down to look at the ground. Dookie Brown smirks. "You can't be hard on borrowed pain," he snarls.

"Who the hell *are* you?" I ask.

The man doesn't stop smirking at Bam. "Picklebean," he sneers.

"Are you from here, Mr…Mr. Picklebean?"

Stumbling across mister gets Picklebean's attention. He looks me square in the face.

"You got a smidge of home training, dontcha boy?"

"Little bit," I say. "Where you from, Mr. Picklebean?"

He frowns.

"Stop calling me that. Mister. Misters have jobs." He smooths out a wrinkle in his left coat pocket. "Here mostly. But I was born in Smithville."

"Why you come to Albany?"

"To get out the country."

Fleet and Bam snicker and cover their mouths. Picklebean swerves his head to get a better view of my godbrother and his cousin.

"Don't you laugh boy. Albany used to mean something. City life. I used to be young and dumb like ya'll. Looking for work. A new chance. Now look at me, in this old body." He pounds his left leg close to his crotch. "Third leg still works fine though." He coughs out a dry laugh.

Fleet shakes his head. "Is Picklebean your real name?"

"It's what your Mama calls me so I'm good with it."

"What you just say?" Dawson's flat and large palms slap the splintered tabletop. Bam holds Dawson's shoulders down. He is the football team captain. Coach Davis nicknamed him "Hulk" for his size and his quick temper. It sat in gold letters on the back of his lettermen's jacket. Dawson was not a middle-of-the-road type dude. He went from zero to sixty about anything that pissed him off. The problem is that Dawson got offended at damn near everything.

"Get off me!" Dawson growled.

A vein throbbed in his right temple. He was hulking up and it wasn't even football season. Dudes learned quick to get out of Dawson's way if he feels you insulted his Mama, his lady, or his family.

Picklebean doesn't flinch or blink.

"Man, just get out of here before my brother gets off this seat." Fleet shakes his head between each word. "Shutup, ya'll." I pat down the air to get my folks to quiet down. "All we need is for ya'll's mama" – I wag two fingers at Dawson and Fleet– "or the pastor to come out here and pray all this away."

"Ain't nobody scared of that little bastard." Picklebean snorts and spits at the ground.

Dookie Brown Picklebean is starting to get on my nerves. "Man, why are you so bitter? You get a nice little meal and – "

"Fuck them meals, young blood." Picklebean slices his hand through the air like he's swatting flies. "This don't make up for the time I sat in jail with them marchers and – "

I hold one finger up like I need to be excused from service.

"You were there? At the movement?"

Picklebean keeps talking to himself, his voice fading in and out.

"Wasn't enough to sit in that jail just to sit in that piece of shit shelter on Residence Avenue. Wasn't worth it." He scratches his chin. "So much singing. Ugh. Mamas, Daddies, Kingly women. Ugh. King. Ugh. Hell. I'ma king." Picklebean scrunches his face up.

"Picklebean." I snap twice. "Picklebean hey."

His eyes glaze over.

"Were you there?"

He doesn't say anything for a minute. Dawson shoves me in my ribs, signaling he was done talking and ready to go. Picklebean finally says something. "I was around. I'd be even more forgotten if I wasn't around."

The back screen door slams and a waft of Jiffy fills our nostrils. Picklebean fidgets with the buttons on his crumpled suit jacket.

"It was hard to find a job as a black man even more back then." A plane drones above our heads in agreement.

"I spent my last piece of money on this suit. Man, you shoulda seen it in the window, looking like it said 'hire him. Hire this country black nigger. Give him a chance.'" Picklebean held his hands in front of him as his jacket sleeves inch up his arms. They were ashy and blotched.

"I went door to door. Smoothing out my suit in the front and tugging at the sleeves to look presentable. Respectable." His stare softened. He looks wounded, like a man who'd given up a long time ago.

"All I wanted was a job," he whimpers. "I wanted to do better once." Picklebean shakes his head and his eyes re-ignite. The nastiness is back.

"Them people – "

"The marchers?"

"Shutup." His rapid blinking makes his face look like it is rewinding. "Yeah. Them people never gave a damn about me or my need for a job. They would walk by, clicking their heels deep into the pavement." He waves his hands low to the ground to show the imaginary sidewalk. "The clicking was annoying. They walked by humming. One became five. Five became fifteen. They started to swarm the street and the sidewalk."

I wish I could download a recorder app for my phone but I had no bars and Mama threatened my life if I add another dollar to the cell phone bill. Picklebean's story sounds like one that the Movement generation tried to hide deep in the closet and forget.

"I got caught up in the swarm. They were on my left and on my right. Slow shuffling, slow moaning, slower to anger than me. One of them tried to link her arm into mine. I pushed my elbow into her ribs."

"You ain't shit," Bam says into the cracks between tabletop boards. We'd been raised since birth not to hit females. Even the ones that thought they were a dude like Shelle Evergreen who bragged about whooping any nigga that looked at her sideways. Shelle even threatened to fight our principal, Mr. Hampton, when he said Shelle couldn't bring her girlfriend to prom.

Picklebean ignores him.

"So what happened?" I lean in. "You got jailed for looking righteous?"

"Yep. Got caught up for looking like them." Picklebean points into open air.

Dawson, Fleet, and Bam scoot down to the end of the table. As he talked, Picklebean grabbed at different parts of his suit: his shirt collar, the bottom hem of his suit jacket, and the waist of his pants. He twitches like he is on that shit. Each memory was an itch Picklebean couldn't scratch enough to forget. He sits on the edge of the picnic table and rocks. I can't tell if it is rage or regret.

"I was swept down Pine Street onto Jefferson Street. There was no way to get out. I felt a pair of hands grab me between my shoulder blades and pluck me out the singing and swaying people. Me, the strange fruit."

I roll my eyes. Strange fruit indeed.

"I turned around and it was Officer Walon, one of Pritchett's do-boys. You know Pritchett, right?"

"Yep. He was in charge of police," I said.

"Looks like somebody taught you something between them two shoulders." He pats the sides of his head.

"So Walon hemmed you up?"

"Scared he was going to drag me away and lay me out."

Stories about black folks in the south disappearing and dying was nothing new. Sometimes people had to talk up people's faces, names, and smells to make themselves remember and make themselves see how anxious staying alive could be. The stories and warnings were worn down and passed mother to son, father to daughter, and generation to generation. Even now, with a car full of people, my Mama and granny refused to let me go to Mitchell County at night. Granny knew a man that had been dragged to death down the highway that connects Albany and Camilla. It was less than 45 minutes away from Albany and I had plenty of cousins and friends who lived there unbothered. "I don't wanna tempt history to repeat itself," she warned.

I think about the folks laid out and missing before me.

"I didn't disappear proper, I reckon." Picklebean said. "They say they jailed me for loitering in public. I had a handful of resumes with me. They arrested me for being black and looking for a job." Picklebean snaps his collar. "They threw me in the back of one of them paddy wagons. Lined us up knuckle to butt. Smacking us on the back, talking about 'march on to Zion.' My knuckles got to know the butt of Ms. Bea."

"Who was Ms. Bea?" Dawson asked.

Piklebean licked his chapped lips. "Bea...Bea...Bea. Lawd that woman was fine. Afro bigger than her pretty little head. Shirt crisper than a razor fade. Her skirt never twisted, even though they herded us like cattle." Picklebean shakes his head and weaves his hands in an out of the air into the shape of a woman. "Bea! Ms. Bea. I wanted to make her my woman. But she was only about the cause. 'For the people, brother,' she'd say whenever she caught me staring at her. Whatever the hell that meant." Picklebean puts his hands on his hips in thought. "Didn't stop me from trying to tug at the hem of her garment. Ha ha!"

Picklebean's dirty old man laugh pushed a chuckle past my lips. More Jiffy and chicken noodle soup smells wafted from the back screen door. Picklebean wrinkles his nose.

"That sweet mess ya'll call cornbread ain't nothing like jailhouse cornbread."

"What's that?"

"Hotwater cornbread," Fleet says. "The flat white kind that we eat on Sundays to sop gravy and greens." Picklebean pushes his lips together and points at Fleet in approval. "Meal, hot water, a bit of salt if you lucky, and a skillet is all you need." Picklebean drifts off. "They clumped us together and I was forced to meet folks. Danny. Arthur. Chuck. Rutha Mae. That one boy…"

He turns his hand sideways and moves it from his throat to above his head.

"That one boy who had the real high voice. I was tired of him singing. One night he squeaked past a high note. I said, 'You ain't in the Temptations!'"

The more Picklebean talked, the more I felt pulled to like him. He wasn't perfect. I liked that.

"We were stuffed in there. Like those slimy sardines and saltines we had to eat. Slimy sardines and creaky voices singing bout the belly of the beast. What we overcoming?"

"Your grumpy ass didn't like the Freedom Singers?" Dawson throws his chin into his cupped hands.

Picklebean shrugs. He drums his fingers on the table searching for a lost song.

"They were alright. Not like my home church Greater Sanctions Missionary Baptist in Smithville."

"You still go to church?"

"God been turned his back on me. I don't waste His time or mine." Picklebean rubs his hands together and pushes outward to wave God away. "Pritchett's lackies saw me sitting as close to the back of the jail wall as possible. Walon looked through the crowd and pointed at me. He said, 'Bring your ass here, boy.' I pushed through a sea of sweaty-pitted white shirts and crumpled suit jackets. They took me to see Pritchett."

"Was he nice?" I wonder if Picklebean will back up what Uncle Clyde said.

He rolls his eyes and flicks his fingers.

"Ever met a nice white man that smiles in your face, shakes your black hand, but when he's with his own people he says we're better off in cages?"

I shake my head no. I didn't really give white folks too much thought.

"Pritchett was nasty-polite," he said. "And he knew what buttons to push. Which sticks to carry down which alleys, you know what I mean?"

"Naw."

Picklebean looks irritated. "It means he knew how to play the game them marchers were playing. He was trying to get on the inside." Picklebean patted his chest for emphasis. "Offered me a job and a steak dinner at South Grand Terrace. It was blacks' only fancy restaurant in this town."

"Damn."

Picklebean furrows his brows in offense.

"I'm a lot of things but I ain't a Tom, boy."

"You told him that?" "Naw. Told him I'd think about it."

"Uh huh."

"I needed to walk out of there on my own two feet. Pritchett sent Walon to come and see if I'd changed my mind and agreed to his offer."

"Did you?"

"It felt good to keep a white man running for a change."

Out of impulse, I reach out to high-five the man with the wrinkled dookie brown suit. Picklebean slowly tilts his head and lifts his hand to high-five me.

"Pritchett came in person to offer me his deal one last time. Hoping that the shithole or the singing softened me up. It didn't."

"Were you there for Dr. King?"

"Naw. Got shipped out to Baker County."

"In your nice suit." Dawson rolls his eyes. Picklebean lunges at Dawson and uses his shirt to pull him closer to his face.

"You know why I wear this suit, boy? Hoping I can still get that steak dinner someday. But every year I settle for thinned gin, Jiffy, and goddamn chicken noodle soup as payment."

Picklebean lets go of Dawson's shirt and hoists himself from the table. He looks each of us in the face as he uses my shoulder to steady himself. "What you willing to drink thinned gin and chicken noodle soup for, little niggers? What any of ya'll willing?" He doesn't wait for an answer. Picklebean staggers towards the parking lot. I reach out for one last question.

"Picklebean! What you think about Martin Luther King, Jr.?" Picklebean half turns his back so I see a scruffy side of his face.

"What about him?"

"Was he everything that we've been told he was?" My throat is dry. Picklebean shrugs. "He was more willing than me."

· 3 ·

BETWEEN THE HEDGES

It was my last college application. Pap demanded that I write the application to the University of Georgia out longhand. I didn't understand why I couldn't submit an online application.

"It's easier to do it over the Internet, Pap," I said. He frowned. "This one needs special attention."

"But Pap it's the middle of the season and –" a large brown hand slips between Pap's face and me.

"Write neat and do that essay right," he fusses from behind his hand. "Let me see it when you're done." I didn't understand Pap's sudden interest in this particular application. I'd applied to other schools without a single word of input or encouragement from Pap's lips. He drove me to the library on Sundays to use the computers. But when I told him and Nana over dinner one night that my teacher encouraged me to apply to UGA, Pap cleared his throat and a small grin appeared on his face.

"Georgia huh? Fine school. Mighty fine school."

"I don't know if I'm going to apply, Pap. I've filled out twelve other applications already." Pap's glare yells at me but his voice is calm. "You gone apply to that school, Reese. Your teacher said to do it, so you gone do it." Pap grabs Nana's hand and kisses it. "Aileen my love? Will you call Reese's guidance counselor and ask him to mail home an application for UGA?" Nana smiles. "Of course." Pap turns back to me. "I don't trust that backpack and all the mess you got in it," he said. Pap wasn't completely wrong. I threw everything in my backpack and then threw it everywhere: into my locker, on the floor during class, and at my friends when I lost a slapbox match. It's crowning glory was a three week old ham and cheese sandwich.

Two days later, an envelope from my school arrived at our house addressed to Nana. She gave it to me without opening it. UGA's application riled Pap up. Some nights, Pap came into my room and stood over me to keep watch as I wrote out the application. His breathing made me fidgety. Nothing went unnoticed. "Hold the pen right, Reese," He said. "Why you write so crooked?" His body blocked out the light from the lamp. Our heads clumped into a shadow monster stretched across the desk.

"Is that black ink?" Pap uses both my shoulders to look down at my desk and squint. "It better be black ink." I hoist the pen above my head to show Pap I was using a black ink pen. A shot of soreness bursts through my shoulder. Pap didn't care it was the middle of football season and my whole body hurt. He wasn't the type of man that you questioned or refused. My Pap, Art Franklin Doherty, Jr., wore gold nugget pinky rings and Obsession cologne. His mustache was thin and always straight. Nana colored his hair jet black once a month at the kitchen counter, usually on a Saturday night while watching white folks sing songs about Jesus on television. Even though he was doughy around his belly and age pulled down most of his body, Pap's voice was thundery and he walked like he had a yard stick for a spine. I swore Pap could look God in the face and not flinch. In other words, Pap ain't never been no punk.

"You almost done with that there application?"

"Yes, sir."

"When is it due?"

"December 15th."

Pap grunts and walks back towards the living room and his favorite recliner. "Stop pussy-footing around and finish that application, boy," he tosses over his shoulder. I mailed the application December 15th at 4:50PM.

***

I hated the wait for college decisions. Like clockwork, I would check the mail before pulling into the driveway after school. Junk coupons, wig magazines, and store catalogues plastered with women in big hats that looked like they could go to my church mocked me everyday. Finally, a large cream envelope with red and gold writing addressed to "Reese Doherty" was buried at the bottom of the mailbox. I remember my English teacher Mrs. Atkinson's advice during senior orientation at the beginning of the year. "Large envelopes are acceptances," she said. "Rejection letters in large envelopes are just cruel." I turn the heavy envelope over in my hands. I fight the instinct to tear open the envelope in the driveway.

Pap needed to do the honors.

Inside the house, I pull the mail up to my mouth to hide my growing smile. "Mail came today." I casually drop the envelope underneath all the junk mail into Pap's lap. He looks up irritated from his crossword puzzle.

"Why you ain't give it to your Nana?"

The slippery coupon inserts slide off Pap's lap onto the floor. The envelope sits proud and waiting. Pap's eyebrows raise first. Then a chuckle runs from his lips. He motions for me to come stand in front of him.

"This what we been waiting for?"

"I think so." Pap turns down the Westerns movie on television. Nana looks on from her seat at the kitchen counter. Her lips part but whisper something only she and God can hear.

"Dear Mr. Doherty – that's right! MISTER." Pap laughs outright this time and lightly punches my arm. "We are writing to inform you that after careful consideration we are elated to offer you a spot in the University of Georgia's incoming freshman class." Pap's yard stick spine bends a little. "Oh wee. Incoming freshman class. Hot damn!" Pap slaps both his knees and sinks back into his chair. Nana squeezes my shoulders from behind.

"That's right you bastards, my boy done got in!"

"Sir?"

"You done punched this ticket." Pap rattles the acceptance letter in the air. I wince as the paper surrenders to his tight grip. I didn't want to wrinkle it. "This ticket I been holding for sixty something years. This right here." The scrunched up paper looks lifeless in his hand.

"I'm not following you, Pap."

"This is the ticket, boy." He shakes a fist full of my acceptance letter. "You the one I been waiting for."

I knew that Pap was from Jackson County, Georgia. He met Nana at Albany State College in the 1950s and never moved back home. At least twice in the summer we headed to Jackson County to visit Pap's parents, Gran Frankie and Grampa Art. Pap always gripped the steering wheel and twisted it when we passed signs that said, "Welcome to Athens! Home of the Bulldogs."

His parents lived on the edge of town at the end of a cul-de-sac named Bri-argreen Circle with our extended kinfolks' houses on either side. Gran and Grampa Art's house didn't have cable or central air conditioning. We hovered around the two big fans in the living room like gnats or sat on the porch with hand fans Gran brought from church. The house smelled like moldy pen-nies and mothballs on the outside. "Keeps the snakes out," Grampa Art said. Nana always nudged my ribs if she saw my nostrils flare and when I didn't say thank you for a bag of pennies quick enough. On the way home, Pap would go through the same ritual, clamping his hands on the steering wheel with a tight jaw. He never offered up what was bothering him. A loud clap brings me back to Pap's smiling face.

"Reese, you know I played a little football, right?" Pap was in Albany State's Sports Hall of Fame for football, track, and basketball. Everybody in Albany knew Pap played "a little football."

"You might've mentioned it once or twice," I smirk.

"Uh huh. Well, I got a lotta folks' attention." Pap closes his eyes and rocks twice in his chair. "Even white folks. But they'd never wanna admit we are good at something or better than them." Pap flicks the UGA envelope.

"Got invited to try out for Georgia's team. By Wally Butts himself."

"Ha. Stop playing, Pap." I knew better than to call him a lie. Not if I wanted to keep my front teeth. Pap's brows raise so high it looks like he grew a new hairline.

"Boy, Coach Wally Butts told me to try out as a walk-on for the team." He pauses between each word like a preacher. I look at Nana. She sweeps her hands in front of her to get me to pay attention to Pap's story.

"Did you try out? What happened?"

Spring 1949
Art Junior peeks into his Daddy's study room. He tries to level his voice. "Daddy, Coach Butts heard bout me and wants me to come try out."

"Who's that, Junior? The coach at that Negro school in Albany?"

Art Junior shakes his head and pushes his tongue against the roof of his mouth. "The coach at Georgia." Art Senior looks up over his glasses. He is a proud and quiet man who doesn't trust white folks. Not trusting whites was a way to stay alive.

"No."

"Daddy, they play good ball. It could get me some schooling and – " Art Senior clears his throat. "I said no." Junior blinks and stuffs his hands into his pockets. He understands his father's hesitation but is disappointed his mention of schooling doesn't get his Daddy to approve.

"Please, Daddy. This is my shot."

Art Senior slams his Bible shut. Worn pages slip loose from the binding. Verses from Matthew and Revelations flutter to the floor.

"Junior, I said no. These white folks out here ain't trying to give you a shot. They're out here for themselves. Always for themselves." Junior's eyes slant downward.

"What about that Negro school down there in Albany, son?" Art moves his hands like a pair of balances. "Or staying here and going into business with me?" Junior's fists bulge from his pockets. "What about that nice girl who lives up the road? You can settle down."

Junior didn't want to settle for Jackson County. He wanted to play football and see if there was anything else out there besides pine trees and fields and watching his father read the Bible.

"NO Daddy! I'm going!" Junior immediately steps to the side to avoid his father's reach. Art doesn't move.

"So you a man now, son?" Art's voice is calm but growing steadily angry. "You gone disrespect me in my own house?"

"No sir. I just want to try –"

Art Senior jumps to his feet and shakes Junior's shoulders. "And make a fool of yourself in front of these crackers? Son, these white people don't want you!" He drops Junior's shoulders and smacks the air upward with an open hand. "Dammit boy! I taught you better than this."

"I just want a chance," Junior whines. He hasn't whined in front of his father since he was a young boy. Junior punches himself in the leg. Whining was not helping him show his father he was a man.

"You go in there wide-eyed and eager, and then what?" Art Senior crosses his arms. "You get on but what kind of life is that gone be for you? You gonna live on the football field?" Art Senior slaps his hands together. "Negroes ain't at Georgia. They ain't never been at Georgia and probably won't be in my lifetime."

Junior catches a renegade tear in his sleeve. "I ain't tryna disrespect you, Daddy," He says into the crook of his arm. "I just wanna do better. Ain't nothing wrong with wanting better?"

"You need to be alive to want something, son." Art rubs his beard and eyes. His son was stubborn, reminding him of his younger self. This was a lesson he'd have to learn on his own. Art Senior sinks his heads between his hands. His shoulders heave but no tears fall.

"Fine, Junior. Go."

Junior quickly leaves his father's presence. This is as much of a blessing as he would get.

The following Saturday, Junior wakes up early and rushes through his chores to get to Sanford Stadium. He borrowed too much of his Mama's scented soap and washed a white t-shirt to wear with his favorite pair of britches. On the way to Athens, Junior flips his hands over each other to warm them up. It was colder than usual this morning. Each breath was hot and sat in front of him as a reminder. *I taught you better than this.* Junior exhales again. *You a man now, son?* Junior pushes his father to the back of his head. Eyes closed, he runs through plays from his high school team. He wonders if whites use the same plays as Negros. The sun smacks the inside of his eyelids.

Junior nods to himself. He was ready.

The bus stops in front of a long row of dark green hedges. No one is around. Junior wonders if anyone black besides janitors like his neighbor Mr. Stevens walked between them. The last of the morning mist capped the top of each bush. Junior tugs at his sweats and shirt. He feels a pair of invisible eyes burn through the back of his neck. Familiar feelings of anxiety about being somewhere he shouldn't be send shivers across Junior's shoulders.

"Hello?"

A thin man in a red shirt and khaki pants with curly blonde hair walks towards him. The man's fingers weave in and out of the top of the hedges. Out of instinct, Junior looks down.

"What you doing here, boy?" the man's question isn't friendly and sounds more like a warning.

"I'm here for football tryouts, mister." The man kicks dirt at Junior's feet.

"You got any proof?"

"Proof, sir?"

"Proof your black ass is supposed to be between these hedges?" Junior fights to swallow the growing hot ball of spit and rage pushing up his throat.

"Coach Butts…he…he said…" the man laughs and he rolls onto the back of his heels. His fingers twitch and grab at the rake in his hand. Junior is mad at himself for stuttering. He hears Daddy's voice. *Making a fool of yourself in front of these crackers.* Junior takes a breath. "Coach Butts told me to come here to work out with the practice squad."

"So I'm just s'posed to take the word of a nigger that the University of Georgia's coach wants him here to practice?" A hot prick in Junior's spine pushes his head up to look directly into the eyes of the lanky white gardener. A spitball tries to push itself through his teeth and into the world.

"Yes."

Before the man in the red shirt could reply, a hand smacks Junior's upper back.

"Doherty?"

Junior fully turns to face a stout man with a white and red fedora on his head and a white shirt.

"Yes sir."

"Coach is fine."

"Yes, coach."

"Looks like you found us okay enough."

The other white man looks confused. "Coach, he don't belong here." Coach Butts looks past Junior. "I'll let you know if I agree, Lou." The man fidgets where he stands and looks at the ground. "Okay, coach."

"Don't you worry now," Coach assures Lou. "I'll protect the integrity of the hedges." Coach crosses his fat index finger over his heart. "On my honor as a coach and as a Georgian."

Lou looks Junior up and down and spits. "Well have a good workout, Coach." Junior smirks at not sitting right in the man's spirit. "Oh! You got two gentlemen waiting on you at the locker room."

Coach steers Junior past Lou and towards the gates. He doesn't say anything to him. Finally, he squeezes Junior's arm to get him to stop.

"Wait here."

"Yes, sir."

Coach Butts walks towards two men in brown trench coats. Junior can't hear their conversation but the men continuously glance back at Junior and shake their heads. With a deep scowl, Coach Butts nods and walks back towards Junior.

"Who were they, coach sir?" The scowl deepens into a furrow across Butt's brows.

"Some flunkies from the president's office. Dirty cleats, they kept saying." The coach talks as if he's in conversation with himself. "This is my team. We need a fullback." Junior nods quietly, unsure if he should answer or wait to be invited back into the conversation.

"Do I need to leave, sir? I don't want to be no trouble."

Butts shakes his head and grabs one of Junior's shoulders. "No trouble. Let's see what you got. You bring a helmet with you?"

"No."

Butts grunts and starts walking towards the other players. Junior takes one step forward and Coach Butts shoves his hand behind him.

"You ain't going in there."

"I need a helmet, sir."

"I'll have one of the players bring it out to you. Go to the field."

"Yes sir."

Junior shuffles his feet in place and hears a pop in his knees. He wasn't sure who was bringing him a helmet or if he'd get one at all. In the distance, Junior hears laughter and joking. The players jog solo or in pairs, looking through Junior or around him to the field. One player with curly red hair walks slowly towards Junior and stops a few feet in front of him. A helmet sat in each hand. Junior braces himself. He wasn't sure what would happen.

"Coach said to give you this extra helmet," he said. His voice sounded like air being forced through a small hole. Junior reaches his hand out to grab the helmet.

"Thanks – "

The other boy's hand snaps back in horror like Junior bit him.

"I don't think you need one though, do you boy?" The red-haired football player bounces Junior's helmet in his hand. "You look like one of these country rock head niggers that run around here." A tuft of red hair blows in the wind like a flame.

"You should be fine." Junior's hand still sat in mid-air in front of him. *For every freckle on his cheek I'm going to knock the shit outta him.* A voice calls out from the field.

"Evans! We playing football or you courtin' Blacks? Give him the damn helmet!"

In his mind Junior sees his father, arms crossed and glasses on the tip of his nose. No Bible verse could soothe the irritation he growing in his heart. Junior knows his next move will make or break him as a man.

"Well, boy?" Evans' stare is icy and demands submission. He never looked a Black in the eyes before.

Junior clinches his teeth like a prayer. A cold calm snaps through his body. He is no longer embarrassed or afraid. A slow, steady, release of pent up anger from unexpected and borrowed places puffs Junior up. He glares at the white boy named Evans with red hair and too many freckles. Uninterested or unwilling to confront the growing darkness trying to reach him through the nigger boy's eyes, Evans drops the helmet and kicks it to Junior's feet.

"Coach doesn't like us late," he says. He turns and jogs away from the hulking black boy with a hardened glare.

Junior turns to walk back through the hedges to the bus stop. He isn't ready to sacrifice the little manhood he just grew.

Damn, Pap.

"Pap, is that why you get so tight when we go through Athens?" My Pap, the man who dared stare down God if need be, softened as his gaze re-adjusted to the present. His watery eyes glance at the piece of paper lying in his lap. "Yep. I'm just reminded about why I missed out. And what I gained." He winks at Nana and rests his hand on my head. "You make your decision as a man. But know you done made your Pap proud."

· 4 ·

GOOD BLEACH

I can't find my keys.

My phone vibrates in my left pant pocket in three short bursts. I don't have to look at the caller ID to guess that it's Auntie Nan's dialysis nurse, Ms. Knox. This is her third call to me today. I shake my coat and listen for jingling keys. The phone vibrates again. I catch a piece of my thumb meat on a renegade paperclip.

Three more vibrations slap against my thigh.

It is my first week at this new job. Even after I spent my last free twenty dollars to take my suit to the cleaner, I still managed to get a collard green juice stain on the front coat lapel while scarfing down my bagged lunch. "You should've used a napkin and not eat like a heathen," I hear Auntie Nan's voice fuss from somewhere in the back of my head. "You'll get something on that nice suit!" I was Auntie Nan's emergency contact after my Uncle Joe passed away two years ago. The phone vibrates once. Ms. Knox left another message. In the first message, she said they needed me to come to the hospital to discuss Auntie Nan's healthcare options. I look at my office door. The keys are still in the lock.

My supervisor's office is in the middle of a maze of joint offices. I knock on the door and he motions me inside without lifting his face from an open laptop.

"Yeah Regis? What can I do you for?"

"Mr. Nicks, I hate to ask but I need to leave early for a family emergency." Mr. Nicks pushes his computer aside and squints at me over a stack of yellow invoices.

"There's no one else who can help you out?"

"No, sir. It's my elderly aunt. I am her emergency contact."

Mr. Nicks flattens one palm at a time on his desk as he gets to his feet. My pocket jumps with more vibrations. "Well, Percy, it is not company policy to allow new workers to request time off – "

"I understand, Mr. Nicks. I'm happy to make up for the time lost by working the evening shifts."

"Are you sure this can't wait until you get off at 5:30? We don't want to start off on the wrong foot now, do we?" His fingers tap the desktop. I try to breathe slowly to hide my irritation. "I am her only emergency contact, Mr. Nicks. I appreciate you helping me out."

"Fine, Percy. But please know this will be noted in your record and we'll talk more about your priorities with this company when you get back."

I curl my toes in my worn square toe shoes and nod.

"I understand. Please excuse me."

Auntie Nan and Uncle Joe raised me right. Otherwise I would've punched him dead in his face.

At the hospital I see Ms. Knox, Auntie Nan's dialysis nurse with thick hips and curves for days. She had to pour herself into those scrubs. I swear she got them one size smaller to show off her figure. Ms. Knox's lips were constantly pursed and her mouth always fixed to say something slick.

"I see you finally decided to check your messages, Mr. Percy Regis." I struggle to look her in the face. She leads me to a chair in the emergency room waiting area. "Percy, did you listen to any of the messages I left for you?"

"No. I heard the first one and got here as fast as I could." *With your fine ass.* Ms. Knox nods.

"Your Aunt Nan's being looked at right now by Dr. Maddox, the chief nephrologist."

"What happened, Ms. Knox?"

"Her blood pressure dropped too low so we brought her in."

"Thank you."

Ms. Knox smiles. "Her pressure is improving but we're worried because the dialysis doesn't seem to be working as well as we hoped." A cold sweat hits my inner thighs.

"Why not?"

"Her URR is low." I sound my words out. "What does that mean?"

"That means her blood is holding too much waste. Her kidneys are only working at minimum capacity."

"This condition complicates her other health issues. You need to speak to her doctors for more explanation and a plan of action."

After sitting through *Maury* – one of the "are you my baby daddy?" episodes – Dr. Maddox appears from the back. I stand to shake his hand. "Mr. Regis."

"Percy."

Dr. Maddox's shoulders slightly relax.

"Okay. Percy. The good news is that your aunt's got fight in her and asked questions through the whole examination." Dr. Maddox tries to smile from the right side of his mouth. It isn't a happy smile. The wrinkles in his forehead make him look like he is shifting through thoughts to explain my Auntie's deteriorating condition. "Percy, her kidneys are shutting down."

"But I thought the dialysis would help?"

"Her urine is thick like syrup."

"But she's been on a stricter diet. Baked chicken, a few peaches and nectarines, no fried foods, and lots of water." Dr. Maddox nods and jots something in Auntie Nan's chart.

"Sometimes the body rejects our efforts to heal it. Her kidneys are too far gone for dialysis. We could put her on the transplant waitlist but I don't think she can last that long. I'm so sorry. You all need to make arrangements." Dr. Maddox clears his throat. "We're moving her to a room for overnight observation. I'll send someone from hospice to speak with you about your options." Tears sting the side of my eyes at the mention of "hospice."

I didn't realize she was so down. As much as I blinked, the reality was not changing. Auntie Nan was dying. And she was going down swinging.

"I wanna stay in my own damn house!" Her voice was high and adamant.

"Auntie, this is for your own good."

"I don't wanna smell ammonia and shit before I die."

"The hospice isn't even in the hospital. It's in a house up the street." She frowns.

"Well, then why can't I stay in my own house?" Auntie pouts her lower lip in protest.

I've seen that lip pout many times over the years. I moved in with Auntie Nan and Uncle Joe on my tenth birthday. Mama was Auntie Nan's youngest sister.

Mama was a hurting woman that couldn't save me from the rough wandering hands that didn't stay around long enough to learn our last name. I was not my own and I was not my mother's. "You almost grown," she'd sigh. "Can't you just let me enjoy what little fineness I have left?"

On the day before my birthday, I saw a small blue suitcase sitting at the door of our apartment. Mama was smoking a cigarette. Her new man was shifting stuff around in the kitchen. Mama blew smoke in my face. "I can't deal with you no more," Mama said. She nods her head to the inside of the apartment. "I'm keeping this one and he don't want no chirren running 'round here that ain't his." She takes a long drag. "Your Uncle Joe and 'nem coming to get you. They'll do right by you." She looked up at the lowering sun in the sky. "Lord knows I didn't mean to be your Mama this long." She doesn't let me back inside the house even though I knock and holler for her to open the door. Finally, I sit outside on the bottom step until Uncle Joe's headlights pierce through the dark driveway. "Hey there, boy," he says. I don't move. He pats me on the back. "Time to go." My Mama doesn't open the screen door to check and see if I'm going with Uncle Joe or a stranger. I catch a glimpse of her through the partially closed blinds curled up on the couch with her new boyfriend laughing at the television.

Uncle Joe searched for all my missing pieces and loved me back together. I didn't make it easy for him. He found pieces of me under my bed with hidden candy bar wrappers and dirty magazines; underneath the last loop of my first silk tie; in snagging my fishing hook in the back of his overalls when he took me fishing out in Sumter County; behind his smirk when I used too much of his good cologne; sitting next to him in church service; in between every dap and high five during a football and basketball game. "I sure wish Joe was here to set you straight so I can stay at my house," Auntie Nan says.

I've sat with Auntie in the hospital for three days. I'm sure I no longer have a job. She reaches for my hand. Her hospital bracelet, "ABNER, NAN," scratches the inside of my wrist. Auntie Nan pulls my arm to bring me closer to the bed. Her hands are clammy. I don't flinch or pull away. I love her. I cover her hands with mine. She turns her head to the side and studies my face.

"Who are you again?"

"Your favorite."

"Hmph."

Everything in the room is sterile. The hospital is drying her out and trying to sterilize her feistiness and laughter. Auntie Nan looks around wide-eyed and blinks hard to focus. Her stare is hazy. A ceiling light buzzes and flickers to bring Auntie back to the room.

An alarm from someone's life machine hollers. The soft pad of Toms and Sketchers briskly walk by Auntie's open door. She shivers.

"Need a blanket?"

"Naw. Something moved through me. Hope it ain't that poor soul in 3B." The man next door was Auntie Nan's neighbor the past two days. He had few visitors but was constantly talking and moaning.

"He settling his business," Auntie said.

One night I heard him moaning through my ear buds, arguing passionately with an unseen memory of a woman. "I loved you more than I loved my Mama's pound cake, gal. Oh. That's funny?" More laughter and moaning.

"Where you going sweetest thang? You don't want me now that I'm old?" The man waits. I yank my out my earbuds. I too listen for a response.

"You there sweetest thang? Miranda?" The man's only response is the sound of beeping machines. "Don't leave me, darlin'. Sure is lonely here. Like when I went over seas." Creaking coming from the man's room sounds like he rolled over on his side in the bed. "I wrote you, woman. Every day I wrote to my Miranda. You couldn't wait on me?"

Silence.

"YOU COULDN'T WAIT?"

More silence.

"Miranda, baby, please answer me. I'm sorry if I made you mad, sweetness. You know how I get."

Auntie Nan opens one eye.

"I wish Miranda would answer him so I can sleep peaceful." She takes her hand and covers her eyes from the light above her bed.

"I ain't but all this one man," he whimpers. Soon after light snoring comes from the room.

Miranda lets him sleep.

Early the next morning, I wake up to Auntie Nan fighting her linen. She pounds her bed with her fists and wrinkles her nose. She is disgusted.

"What is that smell!"

A woman in brown scrubs huffs by pushing a wood handle and a trailing yellow bucket of dirty water and bleach.

"Smells like they're cleaning the floors," I say.

"They don't even use the name brand bleach," Auntie's face bleches.

I'm fascinated. "You can smell a difference in bleach, Auntie?"

"You scrub enough floors and deal with enough chillun you can smell the difference." She shifts from her left to right haunch underneath the covers. "Cheap bleach smells watery and don't burn your nose. You need to use half the bottle to get a streak of clean. It smells like it's struggling to work."

I laugh and think about the dollar store lavender scented bleach stashed under the sink at my apartment.

"The bleach worth a damn burns. It claws at your throat and drags itself through your lungs. It's hard to breath and hurts. That means it's working. If it hurts it's working." She leans over to look out the room and shakes her head.

"They ain't trying to do no work. If I'm paying for to be here then them white folks should use the good bleach."

Auntie looks down at the floor with the snoot of a brown goddess. She peers over her bed and then lifts her face to look at me. It is yellowing and dry.

"I scrubbed rooms like this," she said with authority. "And better. Me and you at night. Remember, Joe?" She tugs at my shirt sleeve. "You'd get off from the gas station at 10 and I'd fix you a plate. Then we'd take a quick nap and get to work." Auntie rests her chin in her hand. She was somewhere else and with someone else other than me.

"We got there and had to go through the back. The hospital people ain't want us to be seen working by the whites. They let us clean the white wing but made us eat and take our breaks in the Negro wing. On the eighth floor."

Auntie squints and searches my face for her familiar.

"The eighth floor was the worst. It always smelled like death. It didn't matter what type of bleach you used." She frowned. "And those black specks! They ain't never sat still. Always scurrying and hovering across the floors." She moved her wrist quickly in a circle. "That's what was so bad. The hovering. The specks moved in a group. Posted themselves up at the front of the door of whoever would die next. Sure did. Nobody but us seemed to notice. People were too busy trying to persuade death to come back later. Asking about medication for 'just a bit more time.' The doctors and nurses always tried to stay busy by jumping room to room so they didn't have to deal with death personally." She smacks the mattress with her open hand. "God, I hated that floor!" She cocks her head to the side and smacks her mouth, working through the memory.

"But I sure didn't mind working on the sixth floor. That was where all the new babies were, right Joe? A flute played a lullaby each time a baby was born. The flute wheezed through the speakers in the Negro wing. We used to take our breaks by looking into the new baby room. You would poke me in my side and tease me about wanting another one." I shake my head and chuckle. *Could I ever be somebody's daddy?*

"Just like that!"

"I hear you, darlin'."

"Don't sass me, boy." Auntie Nan's eyes and the haze over her memory clears. I am her nephew again.

"Some of the people would click by us in their heels and hard-bottom shoes and their suits and Sunday dresses. Claiming to be Christian but not decent enough to give us a nod. Too busy sniffing themselves and putting on airs." Auntie Nan sighs. "You know your Uncle was a deacon, right Percy? Or maybe he was a pastor." Auntie twists her mouth to the right in thought.

"Were you a deacon or a pastor Joe?" She waits for me to answer.

"I was a deacon, my love."

"Ah! A deacon. But you weren't afraid to give them uppity Negroes a piece of your mind!"

We laugh together. Auntie locks her fingers into mine. They are regaining their warmth.

"That boy of ours, Joe? Percy? He hasn't come to see me once! Not once!"

I wince.

"Not once, Nan?" I ask pained.

"Not one time. He…" she searches for words. "He don't understand we refused to use the cheap bleach for him?"

"He knows, sweet lady."

"Don't butter me up, Joe." Auntie Nan waves me away annoyed.

"I didn't deal with them bougie black and white people because they thought they was better then me to be ignored by my boy. I didn't birth him but he mine." I turn my head to let the tears drop out of her sight.

"That sister of mine. She been lost since we were girls. Which I didn't understand because she never wanted for nothing! Our Mama worked hard to keep us in church and out of trouble. Mina just liked what trouble tasted like, I reckon." Auntie looks to the ceiling and breathes in deeply. "I don't wanna call my own blood evil. But what she did to that poor child. Lord."

"Mph, Mph, Mph," she grunts to herself. "This cruel world wasn't meant for black chillun to be innocent." Auntie Nan talks about my Mama as if she's dead and talking about her at her funeral.

"Mina walked this world hoping something good would shake out for her. The world chewed her up an' she ain't care. I took the boy from her to give him a chance." Hot tears force snot from my nose and I snort to stop it.

"Joe, what's wrong with you?" Auntie Nan's free hand covers the top of my hand she's holding. She tightens her grip. "The boy was quiet those first few months. Didn't want me to touch him. Fought me bathing him. Hell, I couldn't be mad at him. He was such a little bud."

I hadn't heard my boyhood nickname in years. I remember having a funny bladder those first few months. Some nights I'd jump out of bed and cry in the middle of the room. A stream of urine ran down my leg and soaked the bottoms of my rolled up pajama pants. Uncle Joe had to hold me down for Auntie Nan to bathe me. His hands were rough like the ones before him but they didn't wander.

"Bud wanted to do right. Sure did. Especially for you, Joe." She taps the top of my hand with her index finger with each word. Nothing's changed.

Suddenly, Auntie Nan grabs at her sides and her face freezes in discomfort until the wave of pain subsides. Her voice is softer.

"Remember them baseboards, Joe?" She scrapes the air with her index finger. "Scraping at the little bits of stuff that folks wanted to avoid and mess over? You hated getting that gunk under your nails." Auntie Nan sinks into her bed and turns away from me. Her head settles into the pillow. Auntie Nan doesn't let go of my hand. "Those nights when I wanted to cry and feel bad about kneeling so low, you'd wink at me and nod back at the boards. 'Keep shinin' them boards,' you said. And I'd keep scraping at the gunk. My boy Bud wouldn't be no gunk. No suh." I smile at her and she blushes like a school girl. She takes her free hand and shoos at me like I'm embarrassing her.

"That boy started rough but he found a way to shine in the world. Shine and shine and shine. Cause we scrubbed him good and scrubbed for him." I squeeze her hand. She lets go and completely turns her back to me.

"Folks are scared to sit and scrub. Scrub until their life is raw and exposed. But that's when the cleaning start." She closes her eyes and reaches her arms around behind her back tracing something in the air.

"Don't get back in the gunk, Bud," she whispers.

PART TWO:
LONG DIVISION

· 5 ·

BEAUTIFUL ONES

We live off of Lonesome Road. There are no streetlights. Our only neighbor, Mr. Janks, lives a quarter of a mile down the road. Him speaking to us is a slight nod of his head while blasting Velvet 105.5 blues from his pickup truck. At night the darkness is thick and has teeth. My brother Stinney disappeared on an early Summer night. It was chilly, like Spring's last stand. The school year was over. Stinney strutted around the house saying "a senior lives here. You better recognize!" Pook was graduating that next Saturday. He was our cousin and Stinney's best friend. Pook's mama Aunt Letta was Mama's middle sister. They came to town after the storms hit Louisiana. Pook's exaggerated vowels kept him connected to home. Girls at school loved when he said "hey bee-beh." Pook's a year older than Stinney and biscuit and fatback thick. Never seen without his Polo boots, Pook had locs with blonde tips that Mama demanded he tied back when he visited.

"You look messy, boy," she fussed after a loc hit her in the eye when Pook hugged her. "Aintee, it's just hair," Pook laughed and swung his head. Mama raised her hands in front of her to avoid being hit.

"Tie 'em up, Pook!"

As usual, he invited Stinney to come to the graduating senior party along with their friend Beanie. Beanie drank moonshine that his Daddy hid behind old paint cans in their garage. I tried some once. It tasted how I thought paint thinner smelled. Beanie thought he was a man. But when he drank, Beanie never came to our door to say hello. He was scared of Mama. And Mama was an equal opportunity ass whooper. That night, I sat pouting on the porch. I was a rising junior and Mama wouldn't let me go with them to the party. Pook grabbed my cheek between his index and middle finger and pinched twice.

"Sup cuzzo? What's wrong bee-beh?"

"I can't go to the party." My lip pouted in protest. Pook laughs. He smells like Polo Red and shea butter.

He calls past me to Stinney.

"C'mon my dude! We late! I gotta make an entrance!"

Stinney yells from the top of the stairs. Mama comes to the doorway. She looks at me and smirks.

"Put that lip up girl! It's not your time yet."

"Why Stinney get to go Mama? Is it HIS time?"

"He's a senior."

"He JUST GOT TO BE A SENIOR! Six hours ago!"

"Who you talking to?" She stares at me from the side of her eye. I shut my mouth. Stinney rushes past me and pushes my head to the side.

"Mama, she can go. She'll be with us all night." Stinney shrugs and and winks.

"Other girls will be there."

"Hoes in training," Mama said.

Pook coughs and covers his mouth to hide his laugh.

"Mama!" She ignores Stinney and digs her hands into her hips.

"Boy, you lucky I'm letting your lil' ass go. Pook too!" Pook throws his hands in front of his chest and shakes his head. "I'm not in it!"

Stinney's eyes widen and his mouth rounds into an "o." His hand moves to the back of his head and pushes it to the front. Stinney puts his hand on my head. He smelled like the barbershop and I could still see fresh cuts kissing his temple and forehead. The razor was too sharp. Stinney stuffed his free hand in his pocket.

"Where ya'll going again?"

"The Springs, Mama."

"Text me when you get there." She looks past them into the car in our driveway. Faint basslines thrum from its trunk. "That's your car Pook?"

"Yes ma'am. Just got it today!"

"Mmmhmm. Letta said she was gone get you that car." Mama shades her eyes like its bright outside. "Where's Beanie?" On cue, a hand waves from the passenger side of Pook's car.

"Uh-huh. He better not be driving, Pook. I know his ass been in his Daddy's moonshine." Like a commander giving her final orders, she points to Stinney and nods. "Home by midnight."

"School's out, Mama! I'm technically a senior now!"

"Midnight. I didn't stutter."

Pook and Stinney answered in unison: "Yes ma'am." They shyly peck Mama's cheek.

"I love ya'll. Bye."

"Be home on time, boy! Don't make me come out. Like last time." Stinney jumps off the porch and throws Mama a half-hearted wave behind his back.

***

12:40AM: No Stinney. I smirk. Mama yells up to me from the living room. "Bring me my phone. Maybe he's texted me." I hurry to Mama's room and scan the top of her dresser. The phone is black and blends into it without the light on. I flip open the phone and shake my head. Mama refuses to pay for an upgrade. I glance at the top left-hand corner. No tiny envelope. No Stinney.

12:53AM: "Sister, get my shoes from my room." I try to find the raggediest pair of sneakers in her closet. *Stinney is really trying Mama so soon?* I hand her the shoes and she absentmindedly nods and pulls them on her feet over her wooly house socks.

"Put your rollers in too, Mama."

"Maybe I will. Go to bed." She shoos me to my room. I hear Mama crank her car and the lights thin out to slits against my wall. I go back downstairs and sit in the recliner by the window and wait. I look at my phone. No Stinney. I send a group text to Pook and Beanie.

"Where RU? Stinney in DEEP trouble."

Pook hits me back immediately.

"At the house. Beanie got fucked up." My phone vibrates. "Stinney wuz at the party B4 I left. Said he'd find a way home."

My phone vibrates again.

"He ain't back yet?"

"Nah," I text back.

2:17AM: A pair of headlights pierces through the dark. Mama's back. Her long legs hop from the car. She fumbles with the lock.

"Damn!"

I run to open it.

"Did you hear me fumbling around with the lock? Why did you open the damn door?" She doesn't let me answer.

Her voice changes.

"Have you heard from your brother?"

"No ma'am."

"At all? Text?"

"No, Mama."

Mama cups her hands around her mouth. A tiny shriek escapes through the small gaps in her fingers. She clinches her fingers tighter, trying to hide her anxiety. Mama turns her back to me and shakes.

"Where is he? Where is my boy?"

***

Stinney's been missing two weeks now. The clouds were moving quicker than usual. In a hurry like they had somewhere to be. Like they'd seen him. I squinted through the cup of my hand up at the clouds over our house. They were flat and confused. Fluffy and white at the top and black and flat-footed on the bottom.

"Gone rain," Mama say.

She looks at the porch floor instead of me. Mama doesn't look me in the eye anymore ever since Stinney's been gone. I nod anyway. Barefoot, Mama gets up from the rocking chair and stretches. Her lower back sinks in towards her stomach as one hand grazes her belly and the other stretches towards the sky. She looks like she is unsure whether to pray or sit down. Her blue polka-dot dress flutters at the bottom and her face shines with a single tear. I watch her from the shadiest part of the porch. Sweat trickles down the lowest part of my back. The place where the shade and heat meet and struggle. I see the whitest side of Mama's eye looking at me.

"Take off those good clothes, girl." Her voice is scratchy. "People ain't coming back. Least not today." I shrug and nod but don't move. The interstate roars to the west of our house. Honking cars, big rigs' slamming brakes, and the rushing wind of traffic over cars barrels towards our house. Urgent. But with no message for us.

"Them clothes, girl! Now!" Our dog Ninny perks one ear up from the bottom step. She was named after Stinney. A low growl grows in Ninny's belly.

She hears something we don't. Must sense more people coming. Mama clicks the back of her throat.

"Guess they ain't done today, Mama?"

"Hmm?"

"Guess they ain't through with us today." I slap an invisible gnat on my leg. Ninny whimpers along with the rocking chair as Mama sits silently, working through my question-statement.

"Guess not, chile. Go wash up. Ladies don't smell like outside. Gone and change, hear?"

"Yes ma'am." Mama smoothes the bottom of her dress. Her slip plays peek-a-boo with me through the inlet of the chair. I giggle at the lace and try to think about myself as a lady. Back when Mama cared.

"Put this girdle on, Sister."

"Mama, people don't wear girdles no more."

Mama stares at me from the end of my bed. She digs her toes into the carpet. A Belk's department store bag wrinkles at her feet.

"You got my hips and your daddy's attitude." She snorts at mentioning Daddy.

"You heavy around there." She kicks the bag towards the door as she lifts herself up to move towards me. She grabs my waist with both hands and traces it. Her hands meet at my belly button.

"You don't need to jiggle."

"Jonesy don't mind my jiggle." Jonesy was the finest boy in 10th grade. We voted on him to be that in the yearbook. He started leaving notes in my locker after the Spring dance. I hoped to meet him at the pool one day this summer.

"Don't be fast. It ain't cute." Mama pushes her fingers into my belly to emphasize her point. Other girls at school were pregnant. I guess it made Mama paranoid.

"Mama! Gone now!"

She pops me on the thigh. I pretend it hurts to make her smile.

Mumbled voices become clearer as I force myself back to the present. Mama is talking to a few somebodies. I lean my head towards the screen door. I want to hear this grown folks' business. It was more police officers. By now I swear we'd seen the entire department.

"How do you spell it again?"

"S-t-i-n-n-e-y."

"I've heard that somewhere."

"Reckon you have. This is the third report ya'll have taken about Stinney. My only boy."

Police been at our house every day since Mama cussed out a police officer and it went viral because I posted the video on my Instagram. The officer was smart at the mouth, shaking his head and suggesting that Stinney "was testing out his legs." He was black and brushed the top of his head with his hand like Stinney. He never looked Mama in the eye. Something poked at me in my lower back to turn the camera on my phone on. "We've had a few black boys disappearing around here lately." The black man talking, Officer Harris, spoke loudly and literally above Mama's head because he wouldn't sit down at the kitchen table. He rocked back and forth on his heels and shared quick nods and smiles with his partner as he shared his theory with us. "Maybe he's not that bad off, Ms. Keen. It's only been a few days. This shouldn't be too much of a concern. Sounds like Timmy is just trying to show he's a man." Mama, however, didn't take lightly to Officer Harris' theory. She watched the news and heard about the missing boys. She knew some of their parents from church or in passing. But at the heart of it, Mama took it as him judging her boy and judging her parenting. Rage surfaced behind Mama's eyes and moved into her chest. Something took over. Her voice grew taller than her.

"His name ain't no Timmy. It's Stinney." She sighs Stinney's name like a prayer. "Go do your goddamn job, please! Even if Stinney wanted to go off and be grown he would've contacted me or someone to let us know he was okay." Mama hops out of the chair and starts walking closer to the wide-eyed man. Officer Harris' hand dropped to his sides and his index finger slightly twitches towards the button on top of his gun harness. Mama notices the slight movement. She stops but her voice marches forward. "Gone and do it. You over here judging me and mine. Do your fucking job! Find my boy!" Mama screams the last sentence. It catches the officer's partner off guard. His blackness and badge didn't squash Mama's anger. "I'm very sorry ma'am," the offending officer stammered. If officers could scurry, that was exactly what he did out our door.

I uploaded the video to my Instagram and Facebook page for Stinney. It was viewed 5,000 times in the first hour and shared over 500 times across Facebook and retweeted on Twitter. "Black Mamas Don't Play," "That bullshit," and "#PoliceAssWhoopinsMatter" popped up in the comment sections. BlackMediaStar, a vines and online video sharing website, picked it up in two hours and Stinney was viral. People were giving at least one damn about him, even if just to laugh at Mama cussing out Officer Harris.

I updated the Facebook page. "WE ARE VIRAL! Have you seen Stinney Keen? Don't let my brother become one of #TheBeautifulOnes." Around school, we started calling the missing boys "the beautiful ones," the ones who flashed across cell phone screens and the single digital billboard on Oglethorpe Avenue smiling in their Sunday's Best and Blue Magic grease-slicked hair. Their folks put them on their best behavior and display, showing that something about them was worth caring about. Even if the boys were bad as hell, like Carlito White, who spit at girls who didn't let him touch their booty and got expelled for fighting the same day he disappeared. Carlito didn't even make the evening news until someone recorded his crying grandmother holding one of his school pictures on the corner of Dawson Road and Oakridge Boulevard. She shoved Carlito's smiling face into every car and person that crossed her path. "Have you seen him? Ain't he handsome? He hasn't called his Maw Maw." Carlito's Maw Maw groaned his name. She made him a beautiful one. She searched every face and car for an opportunity to share something about Carlito that made him worth saving.

The next morning, a beat reporter for the black folks' paper, *The Marathon*, stood shifty-footed on our porch. He said his name was McGillis. He wiped his hands repeatedly on the front of his khakis. Hand sweat streaked his thighs. He reached for my hand to shake it. I hesitated because of the sweat. Mama nudged my shoulder.

"Would you like something to drink Mr. McGillis? A pink lemonade or coke?" I look at Mama to get her approval of my hometraining in action. "Pink lemonade will do fine," McGillis said. I bring a can from the kitchen and sit in the rocker closest to the door. "Always best fresh out the icebox," he says as he wipes the rim with this shirt.

"My boy James goes to school with your boy Stinney," Mr. McGillis said. He clicks off his recorder to go off record. "Ms. Keen, I'm here to get your side of the story. The truth. I heard about your run-in with Officer Harris. He must've said something for you to pop off on him. Got the black ones thinking they actually got some rank under Mr. Charlie's laws." Mr. McGillis chuckles and bounces the recorder on his lap. Mama doesn't crack a smile. Mr. McGillis quickly shifts his smile into a straight line. His cheeks drop. "They won't cover us, you know. Not with everything going on." Mama had a subscription to *The Marathon* and to the white folks' paper *The Envoy*. McGillis looks past Mama at the untouched pile of newspapers at the door. "White folks scared to say 'black,' am I right? Let alone care about what's going on in our community." Mama shrugs McGillis off and her stare remains straight. He clicks the recorder back to "ON."

"Ms. Keen, how have the police handled Stinney's disappearance?"

"Not good enough."

"Oh?"

"It took them days to take a report on my son. Then they come and suggest he was *intentionally* missing."

"Intentionally?"

"Saying he was trying to be grown." Mama rolls her eyes at the thought of Stinney trying to be grown. Or more grown than usual. McGillis nods and parts his lips to speak. The tip of his tongue pushes the back of his front teeth.

"Tell me more about Stinney. Was he an honors student? Athlete?"

"He is my son and missing. Ain't that all that matter?" Mama leans in closer to search McGillis' face to check him out. He slightly leans back.

"Well of course it's important that he's missing. We just want to get a better profile of him. Give you a chance to describe your boy the right way."

"He is a rising senior. He intentionally plucks my nerve trying to wade his way to manhood. He likes girls and his car. And he was...is...overprotective of his baby sister Sister over there." She nods in my direction. "Right, Sister?"

"Her name is Sister?"

"It is." Mama speeds past McGillis' question about how she named us. "Stinney doesn't have a record. Never got into big trouble. My boy deserves to be found. He deserves..."

Mama's voice cracks and trails off. McGillis nods and strokes the stubble on his chin. He turns to me. "You were the one to go to social media about your brother?" McGillis taps the side of his leg and waits on my response.

"Yeah. Police were taking too long and I thought going online could help us find him faster."

McGillis nods. "That was some video you posted." I shrug and Mama scrunches up her entire face. "I didn't want her to put me on no internet." "It worked though," I said. "He matters. Stinney matters."

McGillis clicks off the recorder and extends his hands to Mama and me. "Thank you, Ms. Keen. Sister Keen."

"You're in my prayers," McGillis says.

His steps softly thud into the dusk.

***

Mama called Stinney her "Chocolate Boy Wonder." She had him her sophomore year at Albany State College. She dropped down to a part-time student and then dropped out completely two semesters after he was born. Stinney was smaller than other babies and kids his age and needed more attention.

"But he was a happy baby. Stinney laughs more than he does anything else," Mama said. "You just looked at him and Stinney busted out laughing." If Stinney had a temper it didn't visit but so often. I was born a year and a half later. When Mama showed me to Stinney for the first time all he said was "Dister. Love her. Dister." Mama said he frowned when she told him she wanted to name me Serena. "No Mama, Dister. My dister," he lisped. "He claimed you before I ever could," Mama said.

"Mama? When you file taxes, only file for one kid" Stinney joked. "Sister is always at my side." Mama laughed and pinched his arm.

"Hush, boy."

Where I loved reading and writing stories, Stinney loved working with his hands. On my birthday, I begged Mama for a laptop so I could blog and write about stuff from home. On his 16th birthday, Stinney begged Mama to buy him a car he could restore. Mama bought Uncle Rush's old Cadillac. Its fading blue paint bled into rust. The back door was missing a handle. The engine sputtered but after a few cranks coughed to life. And it sat on cinder blocks lopsided like a drunk man. Stinney had his work cut out for him.

"I'll give it to you for $650 'cause you family," Uncle Rush said. If Uncle Rush did anything in life, he hustled. "And one of your cobblers."

"$350, a cobbler, and I'll pray for you on Sunday," Mama said.

"Done, babygirl. You know I like the crust extra thick. Like my women."

Mama tried to stifle a laugh.

Stinney fell in love with the car. Forgetting all his wannabe grown manness, he hugged Mama's neck tight.

"Thank you, Mama! I gotta call Pook!"

Mama hoped Pook would encourage Stinney to go to college. "You got brains and you're pretty," Mama said to me often. "Pretty fades. Smarts are forever." I didn't need any encouragement. I was 23 of 265 in my class. Stinney, however, needed more motivation.

"Even if it's just community college. Talk to him, nephew. He listens to you."

"I got you, Aintee."

Pook never had a doubt in his mind he was going to college. His dad took him to his alma mater's football homecoming every year. Pook wanted to be a physical trainer. After he was hurt in football he stayed connected to it through working with the team on the side and in the weight room. Last year Stinney went with Pook to homecoming. Stinney was not completely sold.

"I mean, the girls were fine as hell, Sister," he told me when he got back. "But I mean niggas there was stuck up. I mean stick all the way in their ass." I snort and chuckle.

"All the way, brother?" "All the damn way. Pook will be fine, I guess. But I'm not sold."

Mama didn't give up on Stinney being a college man. She said she'd meet him where he was at. One day Mama came home with a bag of CDs.

"Audiobooks, Chocolate Boy Wonder." She called him that when she wanted to butter him up to do what she wanted.

"What are they?"

"Books you listen to on the road."

Stinney threw his head back and laughed. He blows a raspberry. Mama looks horrified.

"Do they knock?"

"Knock what?"

"Do they sound good in the car?"

Mama shoves his shoulder.

"Damn Mama! Your shove got some stank on it like yesteryear!" Mama's laugh immediately turns to an irritated groan.

"Watch your mouth around me, boy!" She shakes the bag full of CDs. "Put these books in that piece of shit car, Stinney!"

"Naw."

"Do better! Learn better!"

"Mama, college ain't my thing." Stinney turns back to the handle he's trying to jiggle into place.

"You can't always do what you want to do, son." Mama winces at the scraping of the metal handle against the car frame. Stinney is still hidden behind the open door.

"Everybody don't go to college, Mama."

"*You* going."

"Don't you want me happy?"

"Happiness don't pay bills, get you right, or where you need to be, Stinney."

He continues to jiggle the handle.

"What if I got my own plans?"

"Like what?"

"Opening a shop. Being a mechanic."

"That's vocational school," I chip in. Stinney rolls his eyes at me.

"So? Still ain't *college-college*."

"You still need to study," Mama and me say together.

"Can I use audiobooks?" Stinney laughs at himself. Mama slams her hand on the hood of the car.

"What about me? How you make me look? When you gone realize this isn't just the Stinney show?" Even though she worked her way to manager at the credit union, Stinney was Mama's chance at redemption. Stinney going to college, graduating, and without kids, would be her pat on the back.

"Let me think about it. I got time." Stinney shoves the handle into the side of the door.

"You burn so bright through this life, son. You gone burn out too soon," Mama says softly into her chest. Stinney continues jiggling the doorhandle.

Mama huffs and walks away.

"I don't need college to save me, Mama!" Stinney yells to Mama's back.

***

After Mr. McGillis ran the story on Stinney, "Stinney Keen: Our Black Sons Just as Important as White Ones," people started flooding the house. At first it was just Pook and Aunt Letta. Aunt Letta rocked back and forth next to Mama. Then random people came by with condolences, food, and prayers. Most of them people just being nosey. Mama repeated the same thing over and over: "Stinney is a good boy. He's only a few minutes late sometimes but he always texts me." She points to her flip phone. "Always texts me. See?" People look at the open phone. There's no tiny envelope. No Stinney. Mama sobs into her hands. Miss Adel, Mama's friend from work, squeezes her shoulders and whispers into her ear. The other folks just nod and "hmph:" Hmph, hmph, hmph. One of them turned to me and reached for my face. I jump back. "Sister, you alright?" I shake my head no. For a brief second, Mama is her old self. "Girl you speak to adults. She asked you a question." And then the spirit leaves her and Mama's face returns to her hands.

"No. I'm not alright. My brother's missing. It's been two weeks. He ain't dead." The woman raises her eyebrows in shock. She looked like she wanted to forgive me because I was grieving. She stares at me.

"He ain't dead! Stinney ain't dead. And you vultures in here grieving like he is. My brother's alive! He's alive!"

I stomp up the stairs. Pook looks at me from around the corner. He steps on the first stair and then stops. Thinking. He nods his head up and to the left towards Stinney's room.

Pook and me sit in Stinney's room. In the silence, I checked my phone and the "Find Stinney" Facebook wall. Comments started turning into spam for money schemes and waist trainers. People were losing interest. Pook sat on Stinney's favorite bean bag. His weight pushed out a few beans past the electric tape.

"I just don't understand, cuzzo," Pook mumbled. I feel a flush of heat and exhaustion. Pook leans his head back into the bag. His locs thud softly against the beanbag skin. "I swear dude was good when I left the party with Beanie. He was...there. He was laughing. Feeling on booties!" I shift to put more of my weight on my right cheek. My left leg was falling asleep. Pook took it as a sign of me being mad at him.

"Babygirl I swear! Stinney was good. He was even talking about college. Taking it seriously. Finally. He –"

I try to jump up and kick Pook in the foot. I sink deeper into the bag.

"Then where he at Pook?! Where's my brother?"

Pook blinks back tears and swipes his face with the back part of his hand.

"The squad been asking around." I shrug.

"Pook, don't lie to me. Are you sure you don't know nothing else?"

"Naw, bee-beh. Nothing. Soon as I hear anything, you the first to know. I swear."

I don't remember Pook leaving but I fell asleep in Stinney's room on the bean bag. The house is quiet. I climb into his bed. His pillow still smells like him.

***

I am at Golddust skating rink. My skates are white and pink, like the pair I had when I was ten. The music was loud and shook the walls but nobody was on the floor. I see a familiar somebody slouched over and fumbling with black skates.

"Stinney?"

He looks up and smiles.

"Hey Sister. Took you long enough." He opens his arms and chest to me. I rush him with a hug and hot tears.

"Where the hell have you been? We've been looking for you. Fighting for you." The music is loud but Stinney's voice is louder.

"I know. I know."

"When you coming home?" I ask into his chest.

I feel his chin on the top of my head.

"We're still looking for you!"

"And that's beautiful, Sister. That's beautiful. Don't forget me. Maybe you'll find me somewhere other than here." He gently pushes me away from him so he can look at me. Half his face was a shadow. He was losing his beauty.

"Am I forgetting you?"

"Nah. Nah."

"What happened?"

"I got picked up," he said. He slid a finger against a skate wheel on the rack to make it spin. "I guess I looked wrong at that party. I was scared. They kept yelling at me and I felt like I was shrinking." He spins the wheel again and looks past my ear into the wall behind me. He nods. "I got shoved into the back of that car. I kept asking 'what I do? What I do?' They told me to shutup and sit straight in the seat. But something felt like it was crawling on me. Pulling me deeper into the cushions. Gnawing and biting at me. Those fuckers didn't even bother to look back. They were laughing. Laughing!"

My hands ball into fists on their own.

"Where you at Stinney?"

"Dunno. But I can't come back."

"Stinney don't say that! We're still looking for you."

Stinney turns me to the side and walks towards the front of the rink.

"I should've hugged ya'll. Should've listened to those damn audiobooks Mama kept buying," he laughed.

"Please come back brother," I whimper.

"I can't, Sister. Do the beautiful ones ever come back?"

***

The next day more people swarm our house. The house stank like collard greens and chicken fried too hard. Mama had three plates in front of her. She picked at each one out of courtesy but didn't eat. I keep watch over Mama at the top of the stairs. Folks tried to come upstairs but I don't let them.

"Your business is downstairs. Not up here."

Two of my teachers, Mr. Bates and Ms. Daryl, stop by the house with my make-up assignments. Two of my best friends, Rheema and Dap, pooled together some gas money and got Dap's older cousin to bring them to my house. They sat watch with me at the top of the stairs. Rheema's head rested in my lap and Dap hung his arm over my shoulder and pulled me into his chest. We didn't say much. They were just there. I appreciated that.

Later that night, my pocket vibrates. Pook's picture on the screen lights up my face in the dark.

"Yeah."

"Come out to the driveway, cuzzo. Heard what happened after me and Beanie left the party." The line clicks. I trample down the stairs past fake mourners and even faker hair. I kiss Mama's cheek.

"I'm going on the porch with Pook. I need some air."

Mama grabs my face and holds it. She looks confused, like she's searching for answers.

"Don't go nowhere," she whimpers. "Don't go." Mama looks defeated. Tired.

Pook sits on the trunk of his car with his head between his hands. A few of his locks cover part of his face. For a second Pook looks like a man.

"What's up babygirl?"

"Tired of all these niggas in my house, man."

"I hear you."

Pook pulls a Black-N-Mild cigar from his left pocket. He takes a deep puff. The smoke is sweet and swirls above his head.

"I know you mad at me, babygirl," he says between drags. He coughs more smoke into the night. "Beanie could've slept it off in the car."

I climb up on the trunk next to Pook.

"Where is Beanie's ass anyway? I thought ya'll were his boys?"

Pook shrugs.

"He don't do well with this type of shit I guess."

"Some friend."

"I guess."

Pook throws his arm around my neck. "You know Stinney is my number one. My brother. I didn't think he wouldn't –" I slap his leg. I can't handle condolences coming from my cousin.

"What happened, cuzzo?"

Pook rolls the cigar in between his index finger and thumb and takes another drag.

"Them Buster boys came to the party." Poppey Buster and his younger brother Nunc were *always* starting some shit. Their family worked on Aspire plantation. Poppey and Nunc tried too hard to hide it. They tried to show they were bout something with damn good knockoff Js and Polo shirts sporting

"In the house on the couch resting," Aunt Letta hisses. "Stop embarrassing yourself and get in this house," she says through clinched teeth. Aunt Letta looks out into the yard and shoots Pook a look. He hops down and jogs towards the porch.

"Put Sister in her room, son. She's out of her head with grief." Pook reaches for my arm and I snatch it out of his grasp. I can't see past my tears. Aunt Letta and pook each put a hand on my upper and lower back to lead me inside. I try to worm away from their touch. Aunt Letta grabs my wrist and nods at the growing sympathetic glances. She mouths "I'm sorry" to those she locks eyes with. My voice travels from my the bottom of my feet out past my chest and into my aunt's face.

"Aunt Letta, give me a damn minute!" The growing crowd gasps. Pook grabs my waist to yank me back from Aunt Letta's scowl.

"Girl, I'm trying to be understanding but you ain't sassing me in front of these people."

"I need to talk to Mama about Stinney!"

"She's under enough pressure as it is," Aunt Letta says.

"The cops know about Stinney!"

"What?"

I sob into Pook's shoulder. "Tell them, Pook!"

Aunt Letta gives Pook a sharp glare. "What you know, boy?"

Like Stinney, Pook runs his hands over the top of his locs.

"I'm not gone ask you again," she says.

"Stinney got into it with them Buster nig – " Pook catches himself and searches for a new word. "He got into it with them Buster boys and got picked up."

"I told you! I told you Stinney ain't dead!" I look up into Mama's deadening eyes. She reaches for me.

"Call the cops back over here," Mama whispers.

A new set of cops comes to the house the next morning at Mama's beckoning. I shuffle through all of the cardboard boxes and soda cans to get a bowl of cereal. The cops knock softly on the doorframe and then ring the doorbell. I try to puff myself up to be grown enough to answer the door with slit eyes and a scowl that demanded answers. I am Stinney's Sister. He needed me to protect him and speak up.

The beautiful ones never come back.

Before they can remove their hats and sit at the kitchen table, I jump in front of Mama. "Why didn't you tell us Stinney was picked up by a squad car?" I demand.

riderless donkeys on the right hand side. But even on their cleanest c
were still known as "them field boys." Stinney didn't care too much fo
They'd had it out before and Stinney whooped his ass after lunch whei
tried to trip Stinney up the stairs.

"Pook, you telling me they know where Stinney is?"

Pook's dreads cover his entire face as he shakes his head. "Naw.
story keeps changing. First, they said they went to the party and left
Then, when the cops came to talk to them they said that Stinney cai
them with a switchblade so…"

"Shit!" I found out about Stinney's switchblade on accident. I saw
his underwear drawer when I was looking for a t-shirt to borrow. Mama d
know about it. Stinney would've *been* missing if she found out.

More sweet smoke.

"Chill out, baby cuzzo. He left his blade in my glove compartment." He po
to the inside of his car. "Poppey said Nunc wrestled it away and he had cuts fi
the fight but when they examined him he didn't have a scratch on him."

"Hmph."

"Anyway, what folks at the party said was that Nunc and Stinney we
arguing. Nunc grew a pair and said he was going to the trunk." Going to tl
trunk meant somebody was about to get cut or shot. My eyes widened. Poc
patted my thigh to calm it from jumping.

"But somebody called the cops. Nunc didn't pop his trunk. He yelled to
his brother and they got out of there."

"What about Stinney?"

"Cops put him in the back of a squad car."

"And?"

"Ain't nobody seen him since."

I thought back to the cops who came to take Mama's statement before she
cussed them out. Did they know about Stinney being picked up?

"I gotta tell Mama."

Pook nods and leans over to kiss my cheek. "I didn't think I'd never see
my boy again," he whispers. I run back to the porch and scream at the top of
my lungs.

"MAMA!"

Folks in the living room rush to front screen door.

"The girl's having a fit," someone in the back of the crowd says.

"I'm not crazy," I yell. I know I am on dangerous ground by yelling and
pointing at adults. "Where's my Mama?"

The first officer, an older white man, turns towards me.

"We didn't know it was Stinney." They knew his name now. The world knows his name now.

"Didn't you frisk him? Ask for ID?" I ask.

"He wasn't under arrest."

"Why the hell was he in the squad car then, sir?" Mama spits 'sir' through her teeth.

"Ms. Keen, we picked him up for questioning about threats at a graduation party. The Springs is a private club and –"

"He was invited to come to the party!"

"Yes." He fixes his glasses. "But we wanted to make sure –"

"Invited!"

The man touches his chin to gain his composure.

"We're doing all we can to see what happened after Stinney was in our custody."

The second officer, a tall lanky white man with bushy blonde hair, touched the old white officer's shoulder to tag into the questioning.

"Ms. Keen, was Stinney involved in any kind of drug or gang culture?"

"What? No!"

"Well when we arrived to de-escalate the situation" – he looks into a pad of notes – "the arresting officers said he was agitated and uncivil." I think back to Pook's glove compartment. *Could Stinney have went back to Pook's car and got the blade? Pook didn't show me the blade. He only pointed to the inside of the car.*

"What does that mean?" Mama asks.

"He didn't want to talk to the police." I suck my teeth. "I thought he wasn't under arrest."

They ignore my statement.

"Ms. Keen?" "Would you trust cops as a young black man living 'round here?"

"The reporting officers said he stumbled as they led him to the car. They noted he might be under the influence of alcohol or narcotics."

"Hell no. Not Stinney."

"We're just trying to get the facts, ma'am."

"No. You're trying to slander my son."

The officers look at each other and sigh.

"Thank you for your time, Ms. Keen. If we hear anything you'll be the first to know."

· 6 ·

HAPPY FEELINS

Granddaddy did not want to come with us to visit my dad in jail. He was a man set in his ways and me and Grandmama were disturbing his Sunday ritual: church and football. I haven't seen my father, Radiant, since he showed up on our doorstep unannounced when I was eight. Mama threw a fit. He protected his face from each blow of her fist. "She don't need a thing like you!" Mama screamed between each blow. As he ducked her jabs, Radiant smiled at me and winked. "You are my worst mistake. She won't be a fuck-up like you," Mama screamed. I'd never seen a man cry until that day. Radiant didn't try to wipe his tears away or hide his feelings from us. Mama slammed the door in his crying face. A few years after my Mama threw hands on him I learned Radiant was incarcerated. I picked up the phone.

"This is a collect call from Primo correctional facilities…"

"Mama! Can I accept a collect call?"

She ran down the stairs and snatched the phone from my hand.

"Yes. I accept."

My ears burned. I didn't hear the voice on the other end but I hear my Mama loud and clear.

"Don't call here anymore, you hear me? She don't need you." Mama slammed the receiver down on the base. She looked at me with shiny eyes. "Mama was that –"

"Nobody," she said and stomped back up the stairs.

Grandmama and Granddaddy are my Mama's parents, but Grandmama seemed relieved I wanted to see my dad. Granddaddy was not as enthusiastic. I remember their conversation after I asked to visit my dad in jail the first time:

"That is a grown man sitting up in there. He got there on his own," Granddaddy huffed from his favorite chair.

"But he's our family," Grandmama fussed.

"No, Genie. He gave us family. There's a difference."

"Well, it ain't Christian like to leave him in there without support."

"He ain't one of us."

"Then I'll take Bezzle with me and we'll go by ourselves."

Granddaddy shakes his head. "You ain't going to that hellhole without me." Grandmama kissed his stubbly cheek.

"Thank you, honey."

"Uh huh." He turned back to the game on television.

On the day of our visit, Granddaddy slid my bedroom door open and turned on the light.

"Wake up, gal. Let's go."

"I'm up."

"That's my girl. Come on so we can stop and eat some breakfast."

"Yes, sir." I rub my eyes from the light and feel around my bed for my glasses. The door to the front of the house opens and closes. I throw on some clothes from my clean clothes hamper and after getting dressed knock on Grandmama's door to be inspected. She looks surprised at the small lumps held up in the front of my chest by thin bra straps.

"Go change," she says.

"I wore this to school Friday and you didn't say anything."

"This is different. Your shorts are too short and you need sleeves." Grandmama tugs at my shorts and shirt to lengthen them. My cheeks tingle.

"But I wore this outfit to school," I offer one more time.

"Put on some jeans and a shirt with sleeves," Grandmama says. She looks down at my widening thighs. "You don't want to bring attention to yourself." I try to cover my body with my hands before backing out of her room to change.

Granddaddy sits in his chair with his eyes closed under his favorite green and yellow baseball hat. A dirt smudge gives the white deer near the brim an eyespot. The steam from Granddaddy's coffee – always two packs of Sweet-N-Low and no cream – climbs the sides of the cup to escape but is mostly untouched. I pat his knee.

"Morning, Granddaddy. How you?"

He doesn't open his eyes. "Hey, sweetness. Doing pretty good. Ready to go?"

"Yes sir."

After collecting my Grandmama from her closet we head out the door and into the van. The sun is still sleeping.

It takes three and a half hours to get to the prison. We always stop at a McDonald's in Macon with a blacked out "M." The hash browns are always greasy but the steak and cheese biscuits are our favorite. There is little talking between us. We get back on the highway as the sun stretches and peeks out from the morning clouds. After a few more hours of cars zipping by us in the middle lane, we turn right onto an unpaved road off the highway. We are close.

My grandparent's van struggles down the gravel road. Their gospel tape jumps with each bump in the road. They only bring two tapes on these trips: Canton Spirituals and Mahalia Jackson. Their Mahalia Jackson's Greatest Hits tape sits underneath Grandmama's arm. She leans to the right against the passenger window asleep. Grandaddy thumps the steering wheel to the tune of "Clean Up." A vein throbs on the right side of his head. His tight jaw chews on a burden. A rock snaps against the windshield and stirs Grandmama from her nap.

"They always put these places out in the country," Grandmama mumbles to herself.

"Uh huh." Grandaddy doesn't break his gaze from the road, grunting and tapping the steering wheel. "Who wants to see these people and their crimes every day?" I look out the window as pine trees morph into metal poles and barbed wire fences over flat land and dead grass.

The lower part of my lungs clips my stomach as Granddaddy pushes the brake all the way to the floor.

We're here.

I knock my head against the window and close my eyes. Granddaddy looks at me from the rearview mirror. "Girl, you ain't sleep." He fights down a chuckle in his throat and clears it. "Bezzle, you ready?" It is more of a command than a question. Granddaddy sighs and heaves his chest. "Yes sir." I pull my knees from the back of his car seat.

Grandaddy didn't want to be here.

The van door rattles open. He reaches out his hand to help me get out of the van. My body pours out lopsided onto the concrete. My legs are asleep and I stumble into Granddaddy's side. He squeezes my shoulder and helps me steady myself. It is 8:30 in the morning. Visitation doesn't start until 9:00am.

Two guards sit behind plexiglass at the entrance. They stare past my grandparents into my chest. I changed clothes into a blue granny blouse with sleeves that barely touched my wrists and a white camisole. Their staring makes me fidgety. Grandmama uses her body to shield me from their stares.

"Button your shirt all the way up," she says softly.

The guards frown as I fumble with the buttons up my shirt. Granddaddy coughs to get their attention.

"Fill out these forms," the guard closest to the counter says. He is short and bald-headed. Dead yellow light reflects off his head from the troffer lights. The clipboard clinks on the counter. Granddaddy slides the clipboard towards Grandmama. He does not break his gaze with the officer.

Grandmama pulls out a Ziploc of quarters and dimes and a slip of paper with Radiant's information. His inmate number is 84070-104. The pen is low on ink and Grandmama repeatedly writes over the numbers to scratch them down on the form. She takes her time, writing his name and number like she was writing in the family Bible. A braid starts to unravel near my face. Grandmama hates my braids but Mama demanded they stay in my head when I visited her this summer.

I start to untwist the braid. It must irritate Granddaddy because he swats my hand away.

"Stop. I know you nervous. But stop, hear?"

"Sorry, Granddaddy."

The guard inspects Grandmama's change baggie and gives her a key to a locker.

"Nothing else goes in with you."

The coins jingle in the bag as Grandmama juggles her purse, Granddaddy's wallet, and car keys. I try to take the bag from her but she twists her body out of my reach. I find three seats in the waiting area. Granddaddy sits straight in the plastic chair, his arms folded across his chest and a scowl on his face.

A faint sound of slamming doors is heard out the window. The air smells like stale coffee. We wait to be escorted to the visiting room with a group of folks. In the waiting area, a potbellied man sleeps with his head buried in his chest and mouth slightly open. His snoring keeps rhythm with the beeping noise coming from the guard station at the front entrance. A white couple in faded blue jeans and matching "Ask me how Jesus Saves" t-shirts sit across from each other. The woman's raggedy Birkenstocks show off her chipped purple toe nail polish. The man's face held a long brown beard.

"Didn't pat my beard down this time," he says to the woman. I can't place the man's accent, but he is not from the South. The woman whispers something only she can hear. Granddaddy looks at the white couple's shirts. "Ain't no need in asking about Jesus here," he mumbles.

"There's always a chance at redemption," Grandmama says as he pats his arm. Granddaddy is not convinced. "Even the devil shined for God once," he says. In the back row of seats a young black woman stares out the window with a gurgling baby in the crook of her arm.

The gate next to the waiting room clicks and a tall guard sucks his teeth to get our attention. "Line up and keep moving." We line up tallest to shortest. The woman and her baby bring up the rear of our group. Chirping birds perched on the barbwire greet us in the breezeway between the front of the prison and its back where visitation is held. I squint at the brightness of the sun. Window slits sit between every twelve groups of brick, some with fingers pushing through and wriggling as solitary acts of freedom.

Another gate clicks. The smell of fake butter popcorn and popping soda can tabs greets us at the door. The floor is cracking linoleum tile. There is a low hum from the vending machines. Men in khaki and orange suits sit scattered throughout the waiting area with their loved ones or lawyers. The lawyers are easy to pick out: mostly uninterested looking white men with shrinking hairlines in black or grey colored suits and patent leather dress shoes. They use their hands a lot as they talk. Two guards stand watch by the gate and a back door with a small white light bulb in its own cell. I am mesmerized by how sad the light seems as it shines on and off. It is brightest when it first switches on. The white light is hazy but strong. Then the light quickly burns out, like it realizes there is no use in fighting. Granddaddy puts his hand on my shoulder, a gesture to keep moving. We settle on a cubby space by the snack vending machines. The light continues blaring on and off, coughing up people in brown or orange suits.

Finally, Radiant is brought from the back. Radiant's skin is like a dingy nickel instead of the electric copper I remember. His hands are cuffed in front of him and his head is down. His bald head gleams under the white light. The hairs of his goatee twitch. After the guard unshackles his hands, Radiant looks around for us. Granddaddy stands up and waves his arm. Radiant shuffles towards us rubbing his wrists. He nods at Granddaddy and shakes both his hands. Radiant hugs Grandmama and kisses her cheek. My eyes never leave his face. He finally stands up straight and looks at me, blinking with excitement. Radiant smooths out his uniform to make himself presentable. His arms reach out to me. I want to be shy but my heart jumps and I lunge forward towards him. A hot tear falls onto my forehead.

"Bee-boo! What's happenin' darlin'?" He talks through his smile. My face is still nestled in his chest.

"Hi, Radiant. Uh, Daddy." The guard by the vending machine clears his throat. I let go of Radiant's waist. He waves his hand in a grand gesture and we re-sit by the vending machines. I sit next to Radiant. Grandmama passes me the change bag and I get a coke and hot fries. Granddaddy wants a diet Coke.

"Daddy, do you want some of my hot fries?"

"No, Bee-boo, I'm fine." A man walks by, his floor-length salt-and-pepper color dreads dragging behind him. They look at each other but don't speak, respecting an unspoken rule to not interrupt visitations.

"Daddy, who's that?"

"Oh. That's Simeon. He's a Rastafarian."

"Rastafarian?" I look at the man at the vending machine. He punches in a code and waits for his selection. Grandmama pinches my thigh. "Stop staring at that man!"

"It means he doesn't cut his hair," Radiant says. "It represents his beliefs. He says he's an elder of Haile Selassie."

"Oh."

"Told you. Jesus don't live here," Granddaddy huffed.

"If God is anywhere in this place, you gotta look for him and hold tight if you find Him," Radiant says.

The same guard with something in his throat taps the metal leg of another inmate's chair with his arm around a woman. Tapping his chair doesn't make the man stop rubbing the woman's stomach and thighs with his hands. The woman's eyes are closed and her head is on the inmate's shoulder. He rubs the top of her legs while saying something in her ear. The woman's legs crack open.

"That's enough now," the guard says. He taps the chair again. The man glares at him and the guard rolls his eyes.

"Wilson, you really going to try me today? After what happened this morning?" The man's look softens and he rubs the woman's thigh one more time. "Don't' make me embarrass you in front of your woman here or tell *Miss Dell* when you leave here." The mention of "Miss Dell" makes Wilson slide his chair close to the wall. The woman sucks her teeth and a piece of her hair sticks to her blue painted lips.

"Who is Miss Dell?" she snaps.

Radiant tries to regain my attention.

"How's school, Bee-boo?"

"I'm starting 10th grade in August."

"Sophomore!"

"I'm in Honors English this year."

"I'm not surprised." He grins and winks at me. It feels familiar but something in his eyes is distant and looking past me.

"She's been reading her whole life," Grandmama says.

"Yes ma'am, Mama Genie! I know she's always loved those books." For a second, the dull yellow light makes him glow.

"Them books are her only job," Grandaddy interjects.

They all look at me and smile. I want to sink into the hard plastic chair.

A man in a white jumpsuit and a polaroid camera around his neck stops in front of us, clasps his hands together, and bows.

"Peace, family."

"Peace, Brother Jenkins," Radiant says.

"Good brother Radiant, might I take a picture of you and your mighty fine family here?" Granddaddy shakes his head no. "Maybe the women folk," he says. Radiant pulls me up to my feet. "Mama Genie, come get into this picture!" Grandmama walks to his other side and places her hands in front of her. I feel dizzy and shift all of my weight into my right leg. I lean into Radiant's side and he takes a deep breath.

"Smile, family!" There is no flash.

Brother Jenkins shakes the polaroid and hands it to Radiant. He waits for a second and pushes the picture into my palm. "Proof of love from your Daddy," he says. We sit back on the unforgiving chairs.

"Tell him about your book report project," Grandmama says. She nods with each word. I turn to Radiant.

"Daddy, have you read *The Great Gatsby*?"

"No ma'am. I haven't." He leans towards me and thumps my knee. "School me."

"Well, it's about a rich white man who throws all of these really awesome parties just to get the attention of this white girl named Daisy that lives across the water from him." He nods and smiles to show he's listening.

"But nobody takes the time to know him. They just whisper about him and believe rumors."

"Rumors like what, darlin'?"

I shrug my shoulders. "He does something called bootlegging." Granddaddy snorts.

"Anyway, he tries to be successful so he can be good enough for the love his life."

"The white girl?"

"Yeah. Daisy. But she ends up killing her husband's mistress and Gatsby takes the heat for it so the mistress' husband shoots him to death."

"That's cold."

"Right? Nobody comes to his funeral." I shake my head. "Everybody was there for the party but not for the funeral. He died alone." I look across at my blinking father. His eyes are glistening.

"Gatsby reminds me of you, daddy."

"Yeah? Why?"

"Cause you're trying so hard to be loved and accepted but keep getting rejected." Grandmama sighs and clasps her hands together. Granddaddy sits up straight in his chair. He looks pained. Radiant wiggles his eyebrows and pops his knees.

"Oh, babygirl. You think I'm not loved?" I lean back in the chair and stare at the ashy nickel man wearing a khaki jumpsuit in front of me. "Do you love me Bee-boo?" his eyes start to water.

"Yep."

"Why?"

"Cause you're my daddy. I was born to love you." Radiant sits up tall and seems to stretch to the ceiling. He pulls me into his chest. His heart pounds through his chest and kisses my cheek. The weight of his world sits heavy on my shoulders and chest. It is hard to breathe. I push him away. He stumbles back into his seat. The guard looks up but doesn't move.

Guilt stings my face and neck. Radiant's face sinks.

I gulp for air. "Is it me? Am I the reason you're in here?" Tears blind me. I feel hands on my shoulders and back.

I'm his Daisy.

"We shouldn't come back here again," Granddaddy growls. "Look what it does to her!"

I take bigger gulps but get less air. Guilt is moving past my face and shoulders into my throat and chest.

"Sweetness, you have to breathe," Granddaddy says. "Calm down." My hands ball into fists and I smack the sides of my arms. Radiant grabs my hands. They disappear into his own.

"Bee-boo what's wrong?" He presses both of our hands into my lap and drops his voice an octave. "Bezzle."

Hearing him say my name snaps me back into that small ass room with stale butter popcorn smell and popping soda can tabs.

"Bezzle. Listen to me, darlin'. My babygirl. My heart."

"Daddy, you're here because of me," I sob. Granddaddy glares at Radiant.

"No, baby. I'm here because I messed up. I fucked up. Me."

Granddaddy pushes himself out of the chair and walks behind me. His hands are hard but they lay gently on my shoulders.

"Tell her, Radiant."

Radiant looks down at his black shoes.

"Tell her. Now. Or we don't come back."

The sad white light blares on and off. Radiant turns his eyes to the door.

"Daddy?"

"Your daddy is a Phoenix Angel," Granddaddy says sharply.

"What?"

"I'm one step above a fallen angel, Bee-boo." Radiant jumps his leg to calm down. He bites the inside of his left cheek.

"Phoenix angels are permanently on God's work bench, darlin'. We aren't capable of being guardians. We don't have wings. We don't have direction." Radiant exhales loud enough to get the attention of the guard. His eyes start to droop.

"We self-destruct on purpose. Kind of like test dummies for God to understand how the world is changing. We just get reborn to self-destruct all over again."

"You've seen God?"

"Nobody sees God head-on, babygirl. But yeah. I've talked to Him. Plenty of times."

"How many times have you died?" This man, my heavenly-ish father, can't be real.

"More than I can count," Radiant chuckles.

"If you're on God's work bench, how did you make me?"

"Your Mama was a mistake." He quickly grabs my hands and shrugs in apology to Grandmama and Granddaddy.

"I wasn't supposed to sniff around your Mama as long as I did."

"Watch yourself, boy." Granddaddy snaps.

Radiant gives Granddaddy a side glance out of his eye. "Your Mama made the world stop. When we conceived you, it was during a thunderstorm. We hoped the thunder would stop God from hearing us." Radiant was quick with a smile and shook his head like a boy my age.

My grandparents were not amused.

"I was consumed by her, Bee-boo. What I felt for her ate me up and made me hot. And when you were born, it was more than love. You were part of me." He squeezes my hands. "More than my daughter. You were a chance at doing something right. Finally getting it right."

"Daddy, I don't understand." I like that Radiant talks to me like an adult. He talks to me like he's talking to himself.

"When I first held you and nuzzled you against my face, I forgot and cared less about what God wanted. You were my purpose." He reaches for my cheek. I put my hand over his and sigh. "Then your mother left me. She didn't think I was a good enough man. I told her the truth but swore I would do right by ya'll. She feared when it would be my time to leave." The Ziploc baggie change slides from my lap. "'Don't come near me or my baby,' she said. The rejection killed me. Literally killed me. When I came back around, she hoped I wouldn't remember her or you."

"Would you forget her?" "I tried forgetting her. But you? You are a piece of my soul. Literally a piece of myself made you. We're magnets."

"Wow."

Radiant waves his hand around his head. "I'm here because I tried smack."

"Like a dumbass," Granddaddy said. "Lamont!" Grandmama swerves her head and looks wistfully at Radiant. "He doesn't mean that." She pats his cheek. "It's stressful here."

"No, Mama Genie. He's right." Granddaddy nods and a silent "hmph" lifts his chest. "What was dope like, Daddy?"

"It was like the world burning through my veins," Radiant said. "Time didn't matter. Your mother wouldn't let me see you. I needed a pain greater than that. If God wanted me to feel the pain of what it really meant to be a human being then losing you was it." Radiant wasn't sure he wanted to be human or heavenly. But he did know he wanted to be my father. And he would keep trying until he got fatherhood right. He'd take as many times as God allowed.

"I'm not Daisy," I said.

"What?"

"I'm not your Daisy."

"That book," Grandmama whispers to Radiant.

"No. You're the only thing I've ever done right."

Something hot sits in my chest.

"Why you gotta be so heavy?" I yell at him and he buries his heads into his hands.

"I'm sorry, Bezzle."

The coughing guard grabs my shoulder. Radiant jumps up and glares at the man. He shakes his head. "Easy now," the guard says.

"Don't touch her. Don't touch my daughter."

"Time to go, inmate."

He pushes the guards hand and forearm away to get to me. "Let me hug my daughter."

"Time to go." He signals to two other guards that he needs help.

Radiant reaches out again but is held back by other guards. The sad light blares brightly then dies. Like him.

"Please, let me just hug her." His shoes clack against the floor.

Grandaddy yanks me up by my arm and pushes me by towards the exit. "Don't look back. Keep walking."

"Bee-boo," Radiant whimpers. I keep walking with my grandfather's stiff hand against the middle of back.

"Bee-boo, Magnets! Remember that, okay? Lights flicker and buzz angrily. "Magnets!"

I turn in the opposite direction for one last glimpse of my heaven failed father. He is flanked on both sides by guards. They are trying to push his head to the ground.

I check my pocket for the polaroid and nod.

Radiant's eyes glisten and his head bows. They drag him back to the sad light's door. The gate clicks behind me as my grandparents pull me away.

I wonder if God was back there, watching, waiting, and taking notes.

· 7 ·

SPLISH-SPLASH

Jefferson Street pool was a small and tired looking white basin with a red brick building out front. An ordinary gray chain-linked fence surrounded the whole property. It had two slamming screen doors with rickety handles. Two bathrooms and a scratched green pool table with one stick, two cue balls, and a missing eight ball sat in the middle of the building. Jefferson Street pool sat on the edge of the Flint River. Unlike the meticulous upkeep of Radium Springs, the white folks' pool that was housed in the back of the old Radium Springs plantation house with azalea gardens and kudzu covered gazebos, Jefferson Street pool had a cracked basin. It was hairline thin but big enough that it lost most of its water by the end of the day. The white folks thought themselves proper to swim at Radium Springs because a past president once swam there to shake the Summer off of him. White folks and their children laid their oversized beach towels across plastic sunning chairs. Pictures of Bulldogs, Confederate flags, and plain white towels offered by the pool staff sat neatly while patrons swam or kicked their feet in the unusually warm water. Smiling pool attendants in their crisp white shorts and polo shirts carefully watched for loose hanging towels and bags and propped them back up to keep the area neat. Even with kicking feet and laughter, the water didn't splash.

It sank and sucked swimmers down, its sagging blue mineralized skin slow to bounce back to form.

There were some black folks who tried to enjoy Radium Springs but the stares and the whispers became too harsh. Local folks said they were the ones who weren't familiar with the bleach in the water from the 1950s and 1960s that white folks tossed in the pool to seek out and eat the bathing suits of Blacks trying to stay cool in the wrong pool. Most Black folks headed to Jefferson Street pool because they knew it was bleach-free and didn't mind its long-standing requirement: the black children who went there every summer had to fill it themselves.

Ironically, Jefferson Street was in Phoebe, a mostly white neighborhood with dark cherry wood stained dog-eared fences standing guard around manicured lawns and flowerbeds. Their houses were two stories, pressure washed, and spitshined. Over arching oak trees and Spanish moss hung over the streets. Streetlights dotted each corner because residents feared too many lights would cause light pollution and bring down property values. Phoebe residents hated Jefferson Street pool. It was too close and too black for their suburb. Every year they petitioned to close it. Every year they were denied. In protest, Phoebe residents refused to let their water be used to fill the pool.

It took a week's worth of water and work to fill it. The children scrambled to find containers for water that came from their own faucets, spigots, and wells. Mason jars, stolen pots from their mama or grandmama's kitchens, buckets, cups, water bottles, even a wheelbarrow were brought to the pool. Mr. Shill, the city council appointed pool guard and supervisor, inspected each container of water to make sure it wasn't too clean or clear. He brought the container eye level and swirled to make sure he saw something in it move. He wasn't beyond shoving the water bearer to the ground if he felt the water wasn't dirty enough: folks said he was one of the original bleach pourers at Radium Springs pool. Through the front screen door to the back, three lines of children worked to move the water. They were careful to not play around too much and drop the water in fear of not being able to swim. One line was for empty containers to be passed back out the door to be refilled. Another line was older kids who could carry full buckets and pots while the final line of smaller children passed water in smaller containers like water bottles and plastic cups. One little boy arched his back to hold his water bottle steady, grinning as he passed it to another little boy in bright red and orange swim trunks and an afro puff tied on the top of his head. The children giggled, sang songs, and talked to each other as they passed the water down the line.

Fill it up! Hurry Up!
Don't Waste a Drop!
Fill it Up! Hurry Up!
Splish, Splash, Stop!

From the back screen door a soft splash could be heard with each deposit.
Splish. Splash.

Some of the older kids came in cars and played music from their radios. Teenagers fiddled with radio knobs to get a clearer signal. Yet above all the staticky clamor of fading radio signals a low boom kept beat, ticking louder at each street intersection. Finally, the boom rolled and crashed into the parking lot, announcing the arrival of Zion Armstrong. Zion, a rising high school senior, hopped out of a freshly washed black pickup. His truck was an early graduation gift from his parents the good Reverend Simon and Mrs. Daniella Armstrong. Zion first started helping fill the pool when he was five years old with an old mixing bowl under Reverend Armstrong's steady gaze. Zion dapped up his friends who were already in line and took off his yellow tee-shirt. Zion tossed it on the patch of grass by the pool entrance. He met eyes with a group of girls from his school. He winked and made his chest jump, a new trick since spring weight training after school. The girls giggled into their towels and blew him air kisses. Zion lowered his eyes and pretended to swipe the sweat from his face to hide his grin. He nodded his head at his friend and cousin, Joel. They both were choosing their favorite girls.

"Help me move folks out the way so I can back up this truck," Zion says. Joel whistles and motions for folks to get out the way while dancing to the music coming out of Zion's speakers. Zion slowly backs up the truck. Mr. Shill throws open the faded blue tarp covering the truck bed and squints from the light bouncing off the water inside.

"Where you get this water?" Mr. Shill demands.

"I used our well at home to fill it up, sir," Zion says proudly.

The rows of children parted like Zion was Moses and the truck chirped as it backed up. The water swished back and forth until Zion stopped the tailgate at the mouth of the pool. After Mr. Shill nodded and approved the water, Zion opened the truck and the water tumbled out. As the sun went down Mr. Shill swatted children away. Between pouted lips and disappointed groans, the children agreed to meet early the next morning to finish their task.

The next morning, across the street and from behind slightly opened wood venetian blinds, a Phoebe resident, Mrs. Pine, sneered and rolled her eyes. "Look at that eyesore," she mumbled to herself. She watched the children run in and out of the screen doors, each slam further irritating her ears. The children, oblivious to her surveillance, continued to sing and finish their job.

> Fill it up! Hurry Up!
> Don't Waste a Drop!
> Fill it Up! Hurry Up!
> Splish, Splash, Stop!

More than anything, they wanted to swim. After five more trips to Zion's well, the pool was full before lunch. Kids gleefully threw off their clothes and tip-toed or cannonballed into the water. Small bits of dirt and grass touched their skins like favorite kinfolks. Their bodies shimmered in the rising sunlight.

As the day stretched out and heated itself up the ordinary chain-linked fence became decorated with bikes, t-shirts, and shorts. Splashing and shrieks of delight echoed from the pool. But as the pool puffed up with happy brown bodies, the water started to sink. From his patch of grass on the side of the pool, Zion noticed the cracked basin sucking out more water than usual.

"Yo. We need to start filling the pool back up!"

Nobody stopped to listen or volunteer. Zion's brow furrowed behind his glasses, much like his father during Sunday sermons. He didn't want to go back home for more water. Heat sizzled up from the cement. Zion didn't notice the two girls with braids, Phoebe and Roni, huddled on side of the pool.

"Girl, this is your chance," Roni whisper-squealed into Phoebe's ear. "He is just so fine. Ain't he a senior this year?" Phoebe nods and hides her face into the crook of her arm to stop blushing. Roni nudges her to volunteer. "Go 'head, girl!"

"I'll go Zion!" Phoebe, an incoming high school freshman, squealed from the other end of the grass. Zion smiles. "Thanks, lil' buddy." Phoebe blushes again, her cheeks on their way to matching her pink and white polka dot tankini. Zion pulls himself up and crosses his arms on his knees. "Do you need me to go with you?" *God, Zion was so cute.* Phoebe wasn't the only one who noticed Zion. An older girl, MiMi, wanted to be seen and noticed by Zion too. She had more boobs in her bikini top and thicker thighs. Mimi smiles and pulls Zion back onto his elbows. "I don't think that little girl needs your help, boo." Phoebe pats her head. Her braids were fresh and her scalp itched. She looks dead into MiMi's face.

"Nah, I'll be quick. Save a spot for me when I get back," Phoebe rolls her eyes at MiMi. Mimi sucks her teeth. Zion nods and turns to talk to his cousin Joel. Phoebe turns around to walk towards the gate. She sees Roni wink and give her a thumbs up.

Behind her, Zion suddenly snaps his fingers. "Aye! Don't use the white folks' water, lil' buddy!" he hollers to Phoebe's back. She nods and waves her hand behind her. *I want him to know my name.* At the entrance, containers lined up like criminals against the fence. Phoebe grabs a chipped mason jar. Mr. Shill watches her walk into the parking lot and turns back to his handheld television. Phoebe looked towards the Flint. The pathway to the river was still blocked for bridge reconstruction. *I need only a little bit of water.* She looks across the street at Mrs. Pine's open picket fence and spots a loosely coiled water hose. Its dripping water licks the sidewalk until the cement looks like a grease stain.

Don't use the white folks' water.

Phoebe shakes her head and pats the braids on the right side of her face. It was hot and she wanted to hurry back so she could be in Zion's face and get him to learn her name. "That hose is spilling more water than I need," she says to herself.

After looking both ways, she crosses the street and tiptoes up to the hose. Phoebe sees the blinds and windows tightly shut. The sun beats down on her forehead until it stings. Phoebe squints and drops the nozzle into the jar. She hears laughing children and music becoming more distant.

Don't use the white folks' water.

The spigot is next to the door. She takes off her flip flops and makes sure to stay on the walkway. Phoebe turns the nozzle to the right. The water creaks and hisses through the pipe. She watches the nozzle jump and water slowly fills the jar. Phoebe turns off the spigot and tiptoes back to the street. With her free hand, Phoebe holds her braids to avoid the tapping sound they would make against the jar. Her flip flops are waiting on her outside of the fence. Phoebe rushes back across the street. Mr. Shill doesn't look up from his television.

"I got some water!" Phoebe yells breathlessly as she dumps the water into the pool. It fizzes like soda.

After tossing her flip flops on the grass and putting the jar back against the fence Phoebe jumps into the pool. Bubbles from kicking Black, brown, and yellow legs kiss her cheeks. She bobs back up from the water and rubs her eyes. She looks around for Zion. He's no longer on the grass or in the pool. She sees Roni and motions for her to come into the pool. *Maybe Roni knows where Zion went.* Phoebe dives back under. The water tickles her exposed scalp. Everything sounds smushed together. She re-emerges and sees two pairs of feet in front of her on the edge of the pool.

One pair belongs to Mr. Shill. The other pair belongs to a police officer. The officer snarls his finger to get Phoebe's attention.

"That her?" he doesn't lower his finger.

Mr. Shill nods.

"Saw her open up that spigot across the street and take water. Left the hose on too. There's a water puddle on the sidewalk."

Phoebe quickly lowers her eyes and grabs her left arm, embarrassed. "I'm sorry, I just wanted – "

"Shutup!" the officer hollers, gaining the attention of some of the kids with their feet in the pool. They hop up and move towards the grass. Phoebe trembles.

"Get out the pool. Now!"

Phoebe looks for her friend Roni. She sees her at the back end of the pool, grabbing her sides. She can't tell if its pool water or tears dripping down her face. "Please sir, I'm too short to hop out here." She points to the steps. "The stairs are right there. Can I – "

"You heard him. NOW. You got too much mouth on you," Mr. Shill yells. The officer grabs the top of Phoebe's head and yanks her up. She screams and tries to move with him to stop the feeling of fire on her scalp. Phoebe's foot scrambles to find the side of the pool and stand. The officer doesn't let go of her braids. He pulls them higher and Phoebe's mouth opens. She swallows for air like a fresh caught fish. The officer throws her to the ground.

"You stealing clean water? Using it for filth?" He glares at Phoebe. His glare shot through time, as if saying "Niggers don't swim."

"Please, sir," Phoebe sobs. "I only used a little bit in a mason jar." Her hand grabs at the officer's fistful of her braids. Stunned and disgusted she touched his hand, the officer throws her to the ground.

Phoebe looks around. People are gathering.

Zion is nowhere to be found.

Aye, lil' buddy. Don't use the white folks' water.

"Somebody film this shit!" a voice hurtles across the pool.

The police officer clinches his fists. Too many Black bodies that are curious about him and what he would do next. He pulls Phoebe's braids to make her sit up straight. He is a vicious puppeteer.

"You stole Phoebe water," he says. Phoebe, still in pain from her tender braids and water in her ears, doesn't understand the officer's accusation. "I am Phoebe, sir."

The officer takes her assertion of her name as an insult. He forcefully shakes Phoebe's head. Her body and head wriggles in pain and terror.

"No, smart ass. Phoebe community water," the officer barks. "Water that you don't pay for."

"Sir, I took a jar of water to help re-fill the pool. Can I please call my – "

"Oh, so you admit to being a nuisance and disturbing the peace?"

"Typical," Mr. Shill sneers. The pool was silent. All that moves is borrowed pool water.

"Get up! Get your delinquent ass up now!"

Phoebe struggles to her feet. Her hair remains clinched in the officer's hand.

"You are under arrest for siphoning water from a residential area and disturbing the peace."

Phoebe cries. She hopes the last bits of water on her braids can hide her tears.

"Stop moving and disobeying an officer!" Phoebe's chest jerks her from left to right.

"Make my job easier! Stand still." He shakes her head. Phoebe continues to dry heave. The officer motions to Mr. Shill. He grabs Phoebe by one shoulder and forces her to sit on the hot cement. Both men's hands press on her chest.

She stops moving.

"Somebody help her!" a voice rings out.

"Is somebody recording this shit?"

The children's bodies no longer shimmer.

· 8 ·

SKIN CARNIVAL

This year Yam promised himself he was going to the fair alone.

He made the decision in August, plotting out a course to ride every ride solo. Every year he went to the fair, Yam was on someone else's time. His freshman year he went with his cousins who yelled, whined, and screamed in his ear in the high swings or on the Battling Ram. Sophomore year, Yam had the flu and couldn't go out in the night air. Junior year, Yam went with Meka, his friend who sometimes let him feel her up just because he was curious. Meka dated his wrestling teammate Gimp on and off since their freshman year. She wanted to make Gimp jealous. "Please," she whispered in Yam's ear between classes a week before the fair. "I'll owe you forever." Some sophomores walked by as Meka sucked on his earlobe and kissed his diamond studs. They gave Yam silent props and nudged each other's side looking at Meka's ass. She was wearing a red thong to match the tips of her hair. Their open mouths and stares made Yam slam his locker door. "Fine." Meka wanted to wear Yam's letterman jacket to the fair even though he just got it earlier that week. He reluctantly agreed.

That night, the cold didn't bite too hard. It nibbled at his exposed skin like Meka did before at his locker. They met at the entrance and Yam paid for both of their wristbands. After one ride on the Himalaya, Meka spotted

Gimp in line for an elephant ear. She pretended to trip into his side. Gimp grinned and grabbed her waist. "Let me talk to you over here for a minute," he said without looking Yam in the face. Meka pointed at Yam. "Ionno. I'm with him tonight." Gimp smirks. "You don't mind, do you bruh?" Yam waved his hands "no." Meka waved goodbye and headed to the Ferris wheel line with Gimp. He held the nape of Meka's neck as she cuddled under his arm and *his* letterman jacket.

"Females," Yam mutters.

As a senior, Yam wanted to enjoy himself and think about something other than college applications, wrestling matches, and his mom's dialysis three times a week. She started her treatment in the summer after being hospitalized for a week because she had back-to-back fainting spells. His Mama thought dialysis wouldn't be that taxing. She was wrong.

"Mama, what time is your appointment over so I can come pick you up?" Yam asked.

"Around 4PM but I'll be alright. I'm just sitting down. I think I can manage bringing myself home."

She ended up in the ditch half a mile down the road from the clinic because she fell asleep at the wheel.

Mama was embarrassed and tried to explain to Yam – and herself – that her condition wasn't all bad. "There's a blessing somewhere in this suffering, Yam," she said while Yam say with her during her appointment. He bit the inside of his bottom lip in rhythm with the machine turning over his mother's blood. Yam already told his coach he would be late to practice Mondays, Wednesdays, and Thursdays to take his mother to the Appleridge Dialysis Treatment Center.

"Strong man," coach said as he extended his hand so Yam could shake it. "You're being a good son and practicing being a good man."

This year, the fair fell on homecoming week. Yam usually went on Thursday nights but this year's game was Thursday and Friday night was the homecoming dance. He decided on Wednesday night because it was the only other night with a $10 all-you-can-ride wristband. Yam's boys Shank and Damon tried to bust his balls after school about going to the fair single.

"Yam, you for real about going to the fair alone tonight?" Shank leans against the backside of Yam's truck.

"Yep. Just me, my dude."

Damon waves Yam off. "Pffffft, bruh. You just don't have enough game to get a date."

"I'm not desperate like yo ass, Dame."

Shank nods in agreement. "True. True. You is a desperate ass. No taking your sister to the fair this year, aight?"

Yam and Shank laugh. Damon sucks his teeth.

"Whatever, haters." Damon points a finger at Yam.

"You got no room for jokes, busta. Your supply of females is steadily shrinking."

"Yam got a supply? Where they at?" Shank squints his eyes, looks around, and flips through an imaginary clipboard. "The paperwork here says all of Yam's stock is borrowed!"

"Aw man. Please." Yam pushes Shank in his chest. "I'm picky." Shank and Damon laugh. "Don't be mad because I don't speak skeezer like you two hoes."

"Sheeyit, I'll be a hoe," Shank shrugs. All three boys laugh. Yam reaches into the truck to turn up the speakers.

"For real though. Why you going by yourself?"

"I'm tired of these girls, man." Yam waves his hand across the parking lot. "Tryna save a little money in my pocket." He reaches for the jacket draped across the passenger seat. "I finally get to wear my own damn letterman." The boys nod in agreement. "True."

"Listen. It's supposed to be colder than a pair of witch titties in a meat freezer tonight," Shank says. "I'ma be ready this year." Yam winces when he glimpses at his watch. He's ten minutes late.

"Ya'll, I'm out. Gotta take care of Mama." His friends dap him up. "Hug her neck for us," they say.

On the way to dialysis Mama pokes her finger in his side.

"No date tonight baby boy?"

"Ma'am?" "No date to the fair," she repeats. "I gave you $50. That is enough for you and a date to ride, play a few games, and eat a little something."

"Mama, I just wanna go and have a good time by myself." He looks at his Mama out the side of his eye. Her neck is bright yellow. "How you feeling? Lightheaded?"

"Boy, I'm fine and I know you." She pokes his arm. "Don't try to change the subject. Are you meeting someone special there you don't want us to know about?" She laughs and blushes to herself.

"Nobody special 'cept me."

They drive by the cemetery. Yam's mama shuts her eyes tight and blocks the image of tombstones and pitched tents covering new caskets. He reaches for his mother's shivering hand.

"You got a long time to stay here," Yam says as he squeezes her hand. "I still have a few nerves left for you to jump on." His mother laughs. "I got my heels ready."

As expected, it was freezing that night. After paying to park, Yam pulls out his jacket to wear over the shirt and sweatshirt he picked out for the night. "Keep that chest covered up," Mama whispered from the couch. "Don't leave nothing be open." Yam decided to wear his cinnamon colored Timberlands sent from his cousin in New York and winces at the thought of fairground dust messing up his boots. He laughs to himself when his breath greets him before it drops to the ground. Yam remembers pretending his cold breath was cigarette smoke as it swirls away from him. The smell of frying oil and hot grills grab his nose before he reaches the gate. His stomach growls hard. Yam walks through the 4-H exhibit to get to the fair entrance. The smell of Grilled sausage and peppers turns to smells of cow shit and livestock.

Why do they always put the 4H exhibits right at the entrance? Yam pulls his letterman jacket tight across his body to avoid getting the smell on his clothes. The smell of livestock sits in his nose.

It was unclean.

Past the farm exhibits is First Mountain Baptist Church's exhibit "Hell House." It was a staple event. The Hell House front door was cracked and peeling yellow paint. It hung slightly ajar with screeching and banging piano key sounds coming from behind the door. The entrance was dark. The side of the house was completely exposed, with blue and clear tarp sectioning off different rooms – sins – in the house. The church spent a ton of money on Hell House as an "act of witnessing" to save wayward souls who came to the fair. They prayed to save groups of lost souls trying to stuff their faces with funnel cake and ride the rides.

The house exhibited all the things that could damn a soul – drinking, pre-marital sex, talking back to your parents, smoking weed, not tithing, not going to church and bible study, eating yellow skittles, drinking too much sweet tea, skipping school, looking a police officer in the eye while black, taking a bath on Wednesdays, not taking a bath on Sundays, crossing the street after sunset, and eating Black Walnut ice cream. Shadows of people in character as lost souls read scripts about how they lost their way against the kickback of a cheap stereo system.

Out front, white folks' smiling faces tried to coerce people to save their souls by passing out pamphlets about why Jesus saves. A picture of Jesus with outstretched hands and two holes in them covered the front of the paper and Jesus nailed to a cross covered the back. Yam waved away a pamphlet by shaking his head. "Jesus, the perfect white man who they'd only accept was black if it was called a deep year-long tan," Yam said to the night air. Each word fell silently and disappeared into the dirt. "Jesus, the one who changed water to wine and dared love to visit even in the darkest basements of the scariest Hell House."

Yam stood in front of the house with flames painted orange, red, and black. A demon gargoyle glared from the front porch of the house. The banner drooped slightly below the standing porch light, "abandon all hope ye who forsake Jesus." Yam was surprised at the number of people in line to enter the house. Some of them were his classmates and giggling in a group humming Christian pop songs. Others were swaying drunk and dipping in and out of line, laughing and burping "forgive me, Lawd." The people in line never spoke to Yam at school. He didn't feel pressure to acknowledge them.

Who wants to see themselves be damned?

Yam rubs his nose. The swirling dirt and hay make him sneeze. An awkward touch on his elbow catches his attention in the growing crowd.

***

How did you know I'd be here...Tonight I'm ready...ready to see you...really see you...I saw you that one time...after the game smoking a Black cigar...looking like Hip Hop...my heart thumped like the woofers in the trunk of the car you leaned against...we never spoke before that night...I thought we could do things before... before I realized I'm complicated...tonight you walked by and brushed your hand against my elbow...to let me know...to follow you...I don't know what beauty is....I don't know how to feel...I'd rather play hide and seek with myself...hide these feelings...what would Mama think...she needs me...and I need this...how do I deal with the fact I like the unsimplistic...you caught me off guard...dipping my fingers in your uncertainty...behind your head...steady...steady...Are people laughing at me or just having a good time....Is Hell really full of smiling and lying white people... Would I go for you...I can't go to the altar....this kind of love isn't accepted at the altar...I can't tell...the warmth of this lie is never enough. Hotter...hotter... longer...until my eyes burn...I think I can love you...Your waves are making me nauseated...I can learn to love myself if I love you...laced fingers...wet aspirations...wet...beautiful...beautiful...

***

Yam stumbles from behind the Hell House tent. His smile is lopsided but unwavering. He dares himself to keep walking forward, to not notice the red and blue denim jacket bolt across the back fence and into the fair crowd. He's still stumbling, past the Exchange Club tables and grilling turkey legs. Stumbling, trying to secretly smell his hands and check himself for strange smells and leftover memories. He is glad he won't have to explain himself or explain to his boys why he was waiting by this particular locker or avoiding eye contact in the cafeteria. The air reeked of cotton candy and shame. Yam trips over a launched skee ball. He still sees the Hell House in the distance judging him and knowing what happened behind its well-meaning backside. The top of his jeans and groin are still damp. Kids scream from the top of the Super Slide. The ground pulls him down like the Gravitron. His limbs are freezing up on him. Yam double checks himself to make sure none of his skin is too exposed. His breathing shallows. He doesn't want to go further into hell. *Why does the devil have time for me?* Yam wonders about whether or not the devil really is chasing down people through small tornados of crisp white pamphlets swirling in the middle of the fairgrounds dropped by uninterested folks who don't know better?

Yam hops into a line for grilled sausage and a candy apple.

I don't wanna be saved.

· 9 ·

AS ABOVE SO BELOW

My name is Janie but Mam, my great aunt, has called me Scoot since I would drag my butt across the floor to grab at cabinet knobs. "Tryna get somewhere fast," she'd laugh. These days, I only answered to that name for her.

Boom. Boom. Boom.

Thunder smashes against the side of our house like fast fists on a plastic cafeteria tabletop during a beat battle. It slides down the wall into the crawl-space underneath the house. My boom box slides towards the edge of my dresser. I worry about the tape recording the radio. Any bump on the radio is a skip on the recording. This mixtape had to be perfect. The radio station is playing commercials. A man yells from the speakers.

"C'mon down and see Steelo at Big Baby's car and rent-a-rim. Four rims or one I'll get that deal done." I have enough time to see if the thunder ruined my mixtape. The rewind button snaps down and whirs backward. No skipping.

"And now, your favorite jams back-to-back on southwest Georgia's favorite station for hip hop and R&B HOT106.1."

I tiptoe backwards to avoid bumping the dresser. A small creak at the tip of my toes makes me stop and look at the door. Mam has super hearing. She hates any type of movement during a thunderstorm. "Thunderstorms are time for God to do His work," she says. I always thought thunder was God cracking

His knuckles. Mam's voice forces itself from the living room through the hall-way and into my face.

"Didn't I tell you turn that radio down and saddown somewhere gal?" For a small woman only an inch over five feet and one hundred pounds when wet her voice can shake a grown man. I frown and turn down the volume. I nod my head for a few moments and hope the next song is the one I've been wait-ing on. "NOW!" Mam hollers. "OFF. NOT DOWN." The door to the front of the house screeches open.

Boom. Rumble. Crack.

I'd been waiting for six hours to record the song off the radio. But I know I'd be working an eternity to lift my jaw off the floor if I tried the feisty little woman probably sitting with her eyes closed in the living room. I sigh and snap the radio off. Maybe tomorrow.

"Scoot! Today ain't the day to live up to your name, gal! Come on in here where I can see you."

It's dark in the living room. A low static wheezing calls from a glow on the left side of the room. Mam is listening to the emergency weather radio. Water dances on the roof. It slides like silk sheets across the front part of the house and skips barefoot across the middle of the roof. Water crashes like heavy aluminum tap shoes down the back of the house.

My eyes reset on the soft yellow glow coming from the countertop in the kitchen. Mam got a weather radio as a door prize at her Poker-Keno Club Christmas party a few years ago (she says it as one big glob, "Pokena"). The radio spits out bits and pieces of information. "Barricade...higher ground. Rain...swells of six to eight feet...this is...emergency weather...advised." The little radio huffs and glows red. Mam bangs her hand on the top of the radio.

"Mam, what's going on?" The rain slams sideways against the house.

"God still working or showing out?"

"Hush, Scoot." She scratches the side of her head.

"Working overtime, it seems like."

"Mam, what if the rain gets worse?"

"We'll go to your Auntie's house. I told her we might be out that way if the weather keeps acting up." Auntie Mae lived on Calvary Road out in the county. It was flat and boring and had only cows and phantom mewing cats. "Flat just like you," my older cousin Spank said one time at a family reunion. I punched him in the mouth and got put in Auntie Mae's room the rest of the day.

"We should be okay though, right Mam?"

"Should be, chile." The house is hot and damp. The smell of musky rainwater creeps underneath the windows and into my nose. The ceiling and floor fans spit out warm air at us. Mam didn't believe in running the air condition. "I'm on a fixed income and you chillun would run that AC and me right on outta here." High pitched shrieks escape from the back room. Most of the time it was just me and Mam at her house during the week but tonight my baby cousins Toot and Hanky were spending the night. Mam smiles on the left side of her mouth.

"Gone and put your cousins in that tub and then all ya'll go to bed."

"Mam, it's only 8:00."

"What I say?" she sucks a long drag of air through her teeth. The discussion was over.

"Yes ma'am."

I'd rather battle the thunderstorm than bathe my cousins. They take everything I say and make it a request instead of a command. "Mam said it's time to take a bath." My five year old girl cousin Toot squeals. "YAS. Bath time for Toot!" Toot overheard me say 'Yas' when I was on the phone with my homegirl Yancy talking about my dress for the Spring dance and she's used it every chance she can get. I shake my outreached hand and Toot happily grabs it. My other baby cousin, Hanky, is eight and pushes my free hand away. "I can do it," he says and stomps to the bathroom.

"Get in the tub."

Toot looks over into the tub of small and limp looking bubbles and wrinkles her nose.

"That's just regular ole dish soap, Janie! The bubbles are so small." I look to make sure Hanky is getting ready to get into the tub. He is playing with his sock. "I want the bubblegum kind," Toot says.

"We ain't got any bubblegum soap here, Tooter."

"Aw." She shakes her head.

"You know you make your own bubbles," I say. She laughs through big hiccups of air. Hanky didn't like the idea of taking a bath, especially with his baby sister.

"I'm too big to take a bath with Toot," he says through a poked out lip. "Big boys take showers!" I roll my eyes. "The last time you took a shower you wet up the whole floor. I had to clean it up, remember?" Hanky squints and pretends to think. I point to the crumpled up clothes in his hand.

"What about those footie pajamas? Are those for big boys?" Hanky's eyes widen and he holds the pajamas to his chest.

"Yes! These are superhero jammies!"

"Uh huh." Hanky puts his ball of superhero pajamas onto the bathroom sink counter. He steps a toe into the water.

"The water too hot, Janie."

I tickle the water with my fingers. Toot is already in the back of the tub covering her stomach and elbows with bubbles.

"Boy get in the tub."

"But Toot pees in the tub!" "Nuh uh!" she sticks her tongue out at Hanky and splashes water in his face.

"Eew pee water! Look! It's yellow!"

In a small opening of bubbles I see some of the dish soap sank to the bottom of the tub. It did kinda look like pee.

"I'm not playing with you, Hanky! Get in this tub and soap up this rag so you can get out quick."

I splash two rags in the water to bubble it up and hand one to Hanky. I wash Toot's back and tummy while Hanky hums to himself and wipes his washcloth under his arms. He slams the rag under the water.

Thunder continues to bang on the house. It sounds impatient.

"Time to get out."

"But I didn't get to play with my toys!"

"Hanky, I thought you were worried about pee water."

The thought of yellow water made by his sister horrifies him. He jumps up and almost hits his back on the faucet. I catch his arm to keep him from falling.

"Gone and get your towel."

"You ain't my mama."

"Don't make me pop you." I flick my thumb and index finger towards him.

"I'll tell Mam!"

I flick his leg. He hollers like I stabbed him.

"MAM!"

His hollering gets lost in the noise coming from outside.

The storm keeps me awake because my room shakes. Shadows play Simon Says with each lightning strike, freezing in place with each brief light up of the room. I push my blanket down around my ankles and kick it off the bed. *I need to cover the window.* Like the end of a magic trick, Mam appears as I swing my legs over the bed. Her nightcap clings on the side of her head for dear life. I see Mam's gray plaits. It must be serious. Mam never let anyone – not even her family – see her hair. "Everybody ain't gotta see my crown to know I got glory," she said.

"Move girl. Hurrup." Mam switches on the light and walks out. The feeling of cold and soggy carpet on my feet wakes me up fast. My naked toes squish through the house.

"Mam! There's water in the house!" Mam is bent over in the linen closet. Her night gown sticks to the upper part of her legs.

"Come help me block off the water with towels." I slosh to the bathroom and grab Toot and Hanky's towels and the monogrammed towels on the rack. I remember the weather alert. *Emergency weather. Advised.* Mam reaches for the towels in my hands.

"Are those my good towels?"

"I grabbed what I could find, Mam."

"Give 'em here." I give her two of the towels.

"Can you stuff the back door for me, sugar? My knees acting up with all this dampness." Mam rubs my back as I kneel down to stuff the cracks of the door. The water is at the bottoms of the floor cabinets. Pine straw, red clay, and tree bark float across the floor. The water is chocolate milk brown.

"Unplug everything! Save the electronics you can." I pop the cords from each outlet.

"I just got this damn microwave!" Mam says. The water gurgles past me, snakes around Mam's ankles, and scurries into the living room.

"Go get the babies and put them in my room, Scoot."

"Yes ma'am."

My rolled up pajama pants are damp. The water continues inching up my legs. Light snoring comes from my cousins' room. I shake them awake. Toot rubs her eye and sucks her thumb.

"I'm sleeeeping." Hanky frowns and pretends to be sleep.

"C'mon ya'll. Let's go to Mam's room."

"Whyyyy?" Hanky sucks on his lower lip like it's a binky.

I try to suck my teeth in a long drag like Mam to get their attention.

"Now. Mam's room."

"But Janiiiiieeeee…"

"C'mon. Let's go build a fort." Hanky jumps up from the bed. His footies touch the soppy carpet.

"UGH TOOT! DID YOU WET THE FLOOR?!?!" Hanky yells at the top of his lungs. Toot's mouth opens into a little "o."

"NUH UH!" She reaches for me to pick her up. I smack Hanky on the thigh.

"I'ma tell!"

"Tell, little boy! If you do that only me and Toot gonna build the fort." Hanky smacks the bed.

"Okay. okay. Can I use Mam's lacy pillows?"

"Yep. Make the fort big." I carry Toot in my arms and Hanky quickly walks behind me. I thrust Toot into her brothers' arm and push them into Mam's room.

"Remember, make the fort big as you can make it."

"With a password?"

"Sure." I close the door and splash back towards the front of the house. I meet Mam in the hallway with an arm full of bedsheets, blankets, and clothes from the dirty clothes hamper.

"Let's do one more round," she says. Mam takes my arm with her free hand to stable herself and walks back towards the front. "Stuff it in there good, now." The water is fighting to get inside. It smells like rotting eggs and sour feet.

"We done the best we can," Mam says over my shoulder. "Let's go to my room." She jiggles the knob.

"What's the password? Yeah! The password!" two small voices demand from the other side of the door.

"Open this damn door! That's the password. Right now!"

The door knob twists and creaks open.

"We made the fort Janie! Like we said we would!" Pillows and a heavy quilt surround Mam's bed. She fingers the edges of the quilt. Her hands were too knotted to quilt anymore but the quilt on her bed was made with her sister and Mama before she died. "Careful babies. This quilt is special." Mam taps my shoulder and points at her legs. I help her swing her legs on the top of the bed. Her footstool is missing.

"Give me that cordless so I can call your Auntie Mae." I look at Mam's clock on the nightstand. It glows 1:48AM. Mam's fingers push some of the numbers together so they make a loud screech.

"Hey Mae? Yeah. Mmhmm. A little water got in." Hanky and Toot jump on the bed. Mam waves her hand to get them to settle down. "No, we fine." They continue to hop up and down, making sure their feet don't leave the bed.

"Naw. We fine. The water ain't too high." Mam reaches over me and pokes her fingers through the blinds. A lone streetlight flickers outside her window. "I haven't looked out at the cemetery. She pulls the phone from her ear and frowns at it. A long murmur is heard from the receiver. "Naw. I don't wanna see if it's still there, Mae!"

Mam lives in front of Roselawn Estates, the white folks' cemetery. It overlooks the river and has manicured green grass and tall white marble statues. People bought benches along with their plots so they could look at the river when they came to visit their loved ones. Black folks were buried further down the street at Sweetwood Memorial Gardens. Mam said she bought the house to piss off the white folks.

"Lord, them people had a fit when they saw this ole black lady sitting on the porch waving at they processionals," she laughed. "They didn't want my company in this life but I am going to wave 'em on into the next one," Mam says. "They gotta remember black folks one mo' gain before they can rest," she'd laugh. "White folks busy, you know? Scrambling to make sure black folks are on the run-around. Wouldn't you be tired too?"

Mam shakes her hand at Hanky and Toot and points down at the bed. "Uh-huh. We'll wait in my room for ya'll with the truck. Tell Boone don't be taking all day. Okay now. Bye-bye." Toot looks over the bed with wide eyes.

"Mam! Mam look!" She points over the edge of the bed with two short index fingers. "Crunchy chocolate milk!"

Twigs and branches creep across Mam's floor. They move quietly and in pairs, tumbling over each other and into the bed legs. The wind tries to whisper in our ears from outside. There is a soft thud against the other side of the door.

"Can I drink some?"

"Not if you want to get sick," Mam says. "Now be a big girl and protect the fort."

"By any means!" Hanky yells.

"Boy, use your inside voice. Protect the fort quietly."

"By any meansssss," Hanky mouths. He chews on the "s." The ruffled duster on Mam's bed jumps from peach to a brick red. My head slides onto her shoulder.

"Mam, the water's higher." She kisses my forehead.

"Them towels holding, Scoot. They can hold a bit longer." I search through the blankets for Mam's hand. "We're okay up here."

"What about my mixtapes?"

"Your what now?" "My mixtapes. The songs I record off the radio." "That racket." Mam shakes her head. "You stay put."

"Yeah, Janie, stay put! Don't you see the gators in the moat?" Toot points in the dark to nothing.

Ain't no gators, silly girl.

Mam nudges my side. "Play along," she hisses.

I cover my mouth with my hands. They're damp from the water crawling up Mam's bed covers. I wonder about my tapes. They are my life. Most were scrawled in fading black ink on peeling label paper that flipped up on the edges. I wonder if they're clinking against each other as they float through the house, making their own new mixes. Parts of myself are searching for me. I hope I don't easily wash out. I shake my watch to get it to glow in the dark.

It's 4:23AM.

The phone rings. My finger tips push the phone further away. I use my foot to kick it back towards Mam. Auntie Mae's voice is grainy and small from the holes in the receiver.

"Ya'll stop playing and pick up this phone! Hello?"

Mam breathes heavy as she moves a sleeping Hanky off of her arm. "These chillun gain a hundred pounds when they sleep," she huffs. "This boy's heavy as a sack of onions." Mam takes another coughy breath. I can tell she used to smoke. "Help your Mam, Scoot! Gimme the phone." Auntie Mae is still fussing on the other end "Ya'll alright over there? Hello?"

"Yeah Mae?"

"Boone coming over in the next half and hour or so. They been sandbagging the back end of our street. Not the front end, though." Mam nods like she's talking to Auntie Mae in person. "Boone's coming, hear?"

"I hear you," Mam says. "We here on the bed in my room. The water is trying to come over the side of the bed." Muddy waters grip the end of the quilt and are tickled by flood water. Toot and Hanky are still sleep, holding each other up. Toot snores like a grown man. A pig tail falls slides from underneath her night cap and sits in the front of her face. Sunshine peeks through the window. The water stands tall, waiting.

"Mam, is this God still doing his work?"

I flinch in instinct at the possibility of Mam whooping me. She hadn't whooped me in a long time but I didn't put it past her. Mam doesn't like me to ask her what she calls "grown folks questions." When I was nine years old, I got the ass whooping of my life when I asked her about whether not Jesus was ashy. "He lived in the desert for 40 days, right Mam?" She nodded. "Did he get ashy?" Mam's eyes grew wide and my behind stung before I blinked. "God ain't trife and you shouldn't be neither," she'd say.

"Mam?"

She slaps the quilts like a warning. "God's work ain't for us to judge, gal." Mam always seems so sure. The yellow white sunlight fights with swirling red and blue lights to peek through Mam's velvet curtains. A different rumbling marches down our street. Mam moves Toot's body from her side to my lap. She sucks in air from her teeth as her feet touch the water.

"Shit!"

Silent red and blue lights push Mam towards the door. She hums "How I Got Over." Hanky groans and whines to get underneath my arm. Water gurgles through Mam's legs and into the room.

"Mam, you need me?"

"Watch the little ones, sugar." The hallway is dark and wet. The squeaky spot that usually sits underneath the hallway carpet runner is silent. I wait for the door to slosh open. Toot rolls over on Hanky's back freeing my arm. A tingle shoots through my arm and stops next to my heart. My chattering teeth block out the sound of my splashing legs. Photos sticking to cracked glass and splintered wood frames are distorted by trapped air bubbles. Mam is swallowed by hazy red glow. She looks like an angel hiding from an angry God.

"Uncle Boone out there, Mam?"

"Hoping so, baby." She threads the blinds' string between her fingers to look. God's glare drops from bright red to cool blue.

Picture frames, *Jet* magazines, and a month's worth of church bulletins float by our ankles. Mam opens the door. Water doesn't rush out but welcomes itself in.

"Boone! You out there boy?"

A soft jingle from an open car door answers her. Uncle Boone is halfway out of his truck. He's staring at the door but not moving. A gleam makes me and Mam look down in the water.

"Jesus," she whispers. A silver and blue casket bumps against the doorframe near

Mam's bare legs. It keeps beat with Uncle Boone's jingling truck.

PART THREE:
STITCHES IN TIME

· 1 0 ·

THE APOTHECARY

Band camp started on a Wednesday, two weeks before I started my freshman year of high school. My stomach turned and jumped that morning. I threw up my breakfast. Mama gave me a coke and told me to sit down.

"It's okay to be nervous," she said.

In middle school I was the first chair clarinet in Mr. Barnett's advanced band. I wanted to try out for the marching band because of my cousin, Drea. "Marching band keeps you busy and everybody knows that people come for the 5th quarter."

"What's the 5th quarter?"

Drea shakes her head. "The only part of the game that matters. When the bands battle. You better come correct." Drea played the tenor sax and was the only girl on the saxophone line. She took it serious and made sure I knew she wouldn't rescue me. "You gotta show and prove, youngin'."

Drea got her license the week before on her birthday and offered to drive me to the first day of camp. My daddy refused. "We'll take her. I want to talk to the director and ask a few questions." Drea shrugs and shoots me an "I tried" look. We both knew what daddy *really* wanted to do: check out the boys and let them see I was *his* daughter.

That morning, music blasted from open car doors and trunks. Kids were laughing, hugging, and catching up from the summer. Some of the former band members who just graduated in May came out for the first day. I search the growing crowd of band folks for Drea. She is sitting on the back of her car talking to some boy with her instrument case jumping in her lap. She waves and hops off the car. We didn't get to talk because of a long blowing whistle. Two boys and a girl blow their whistles and motion towards the field. The girl spoke first.

"You know what it is! Vets on the field and frosh on the track!"

"Frosh?" I whisper to Drea. She shakes her head. "Shh. Frosh is freshman," Drea says through her teeth. "Don't talk unless the drum majors speak to you first or you gotta run laps." Drea pushes me towards the other freshmen and I jog to the field. One of the boy drum majors is on the football field that is in the middle of the running track. He is tall. His ankle socks slip off his ankles into his classics. I thought his voice would be high but when he yelled it was a low rumble.

"Six laps! As a warm up!" We start to jog. He looks irritated. "When I say something you respond 'yes sir' or 'no sir!' Am I clear?" We holler in unison "yes sir! Drum major sir!"

The sun rises high and slaps us across our backs, chests, and bare legs. One girl's nose started to bleed after the second lap and her grandmother rushed her to the emergency room. Marching was hard! I couldn't lift my knees high enough or bend them to the right angle. The skinny drum major, Stylus Majors, was always in my face and catching every mistake. I caught myself looking at the saxophone section every few minutes. Drea didn't look in my direction. I missed another cue to turn.

"Frosh! Pay attention and get them knees up." Stylus points at my wobbly leg trying to stay in the air. "Your knees ain't high enough. You're messing up the whole line."

"Sorry, sir!" I try to hike my knee higher and hit my elbow. I tumble into Stylus' open chest. The vets of my section swallow their laughs and stare ahead. I flop around like a caught fish trying to stand on my own. "Sorry, Drum Major," I mumble. "Get it together," Stylus said. "Guess you need more conditioning. Give me twenty pushups and a lap." Jogging around the track, Stylus stands in the same spot as morning warm-ups like a drill sergeant. His arms are crossed behind his back. A voice hollers his name. "Majors AKA Shawty Slim! What's good though?" A boy with hulking shoulders and a gut poking out from under his three-sizes-too small mesh jersey drops his helmet at Stylus' feet. He laughs and daps up the football player. "Can't call it." He nods in my direction. "Out here tryna get that new blood to act right." The massive boy looks in my direction and waves. "Get 'em right get 'em tight!" he yells. Heat and gnats hover around my lower legs. "Handle that," the football player winks and swats a lone mosquito from the front of his face. He turns to leave. "Glad ya'll out here practicing them squeaks and whistles. Maybe people will actually stay to hear ya'll this year." Stylus rolls his eyes. "Whatever. You know people come for the band." The football player shakes his head, laughs, and pushes his helmet on his head. He does a heavy shuffle towards the other players doing jumping jacks. Stylus blows his whistle. "Pick up the pace frosh! I ain't got all day!"

I slow down to a stroll.

"Hurry up!"

"I'm almost done."

Stylus jogs from the center of the field and starts to walk with me.

"Not on my watch." He pushes my shoulder. "Let's go! Move!"

"Boy, get off me!" The shriek in my voice catches Stylus off guard. He wipes his hands on his shorts and turns his head. "Don't push me!" The band director, Mr. Swiss, looks up from the table where he's working through field formations.

"Majors! This isn't a good look for running your first band camp as drum major, son! The band is supposed to be ready and warmed up. All I hear is out of tune horns and off key woodwinds!" Mr. Swiss punches the table with his finger at the end of each sentence. "Majors! You hear me? You and that girl get to moving! Just because the sun isn't forgiving means I will be!"

Stylus twists the waistband on his basketball shorts and pulls his fitted hat down over his eyes.

"Yes sir!" He glares at me from underneath the slightly raised brim. He grabs my arm and pulls me to him. He whisper spits in my ear.

"Cut the bullshit," he hisses. "Get the lead out your ass and move or get out of my camp." Mr. Swiss stands with one leg on the bench in front of the table.

"Mr. Majors! Live up to your last name!"

I am grateful for our lunch break. Cars full of loud upperclassmen peel out of the parking lot hitting every pothole and bump in the uneven pavement. The sound of scratching metal and bass from speakers echo back to me. A small wind blows and I sigh under the lone tree by the band room. Daddy gave me a stern warning about going off campus for lunch.

"No cars." He stretched out his fingers to count. "I don't care if Drea or CeeCee or Jobo or whoever gets in the car. You stay at the school." Daddy didn't care if he embarrassed me or not. One time, I missed curfew sitting on the steps at a friend's house down the street from us. Daddy found the holiest shirt he owned and a pair of bicycle shorts to drag me home. Besides, Drea promised to bring me back a fried chicken sandwich and fries. Clicking cleats and grunts float from the football practice field. I pick up my folder of music and start humming my section. Mr. Swiss wanted this piece memorized by Friday. A car speeds by the school and thumps a familiar beat. I start beatboxing along with it.

"You sure you're in the right section, frosh?" a deep voice creeps up behind me. I jump before I regain my cool to shrug my shoulders. Stylus chuckles under his breath.

"Maybe not, sir." I try and say 'sir' like my Mama when she's mad at Daddy. Stylus grins.

"We're on break. You can call me Stylus."

"Whatever."

Stylus sits next to me on the band stoop and stretches his matchstick legs out in front of him. He smells like fresh laundry and CK One. I scoot away from him.

"You like marching band so far?"

"Hell naw." I didn't like the way I sounded when I tried to cuss. But I perfected "hell naw" after watching enough *Color Purple* and listening to my aunties at cookouts after they had too much to drink. "You suck as a drum major."

"Oh!" He throws his head back and laughs. "I'm doing my job."

I turn to face him and give him a piece of my mind. "Why you always harassing me?" I point to the empty field. "There are tons of other freshman out there messing up and– "

"They don't have a dimple like you."

He reaches over my lap and grabs my open bag of chips.

"I don't play about my BBQ chips, sir!" He tickles my sides. The places he touches tingle and shoot down the side of my body. The kickback of rusty exhaust pipes and hip hop carry in the air. Stylus jumps up and digs his whistle out of his pocket.

"Back at it," he says and walks back into the band room. A blast of air conditioning hits my face. He winks. "Come help me set up for afternoon rehearsal."

Everyday afterward I make sure to grab an extra bag of BBQ chips for Stylus for our lunches on the back steps. One of the percussion section leaders, C.B., stopped in front of us in his hurry to lunch. He looks me over. "Aye, Majors, she must be something special." I can't tell if the heat in my cheeks is from the August sun or somewhere inside of me. Stylus nods. "She aight," he says and pokes my thigh. "Her beat boxing is mean though!" C.B. yells. "Okay! Okay! I'ma see bout you when I get back." He jiggles my knee and smiles. "I was worried bout you, Styles" he swings his head in Stylus' direction. "You ever gone say my name right?" Stylus asks. C.B. shrugs. "Nah." He looks back to me and nods. "If she can beatbox it doesn't matter if she got a bubble or not." Stylus jumps up and pushes C.B. off the bottom step. They laugh.

"Don't pay that fool no mind," Stylus says. I'd never seen a boy blush. He tears open his bag of chips. "What classes you taking this year?"

"I got honors English, Civics, Algebra, Spanish, and Band."

"Yeah? You got Wayland for Civics?"

"I think so."

"Watch him. He likes to talk down to black students." Something darkens behind his eyes. He looks out at the parking lot.

"I got kicked out of the gifted program because of that crack –" he stomps his feet and pulls his arms behind his head. "Anyway, be careful." I grab at his lifted arms to calm him down.

"So is marching music the only kind you like?" He sighs like he's in love. "Music is my life, girl." He tells me he's been playing instruments since he was seven. "I play saxophone in concert band in the off season and trumpet for my church on third and fourth Sundays." He sounds like a professional musician. *In the offseason.* "I think I'm going to start piano lessons this year after marching band is over." His legs jump in front of him like he's in thought. "Any time to breathe?" I ask.

"It's my life, girl," he says again.

Stylus would call me everyday after camp at 8:30PM. I thanked God I had my own line. After dinner, daddy would watch me run up stairs to make sure I caught the ringing phone. His body ate up most of my open doorframe – I couldn't shut my door unless I was changing clothes or after a shower – and if he wasn't standing in my door his heavy steps passed by my room more often.

"No boyfriends, miss lady." Daddy had the only voice deeper than Stylus but it didn't make me swoon. "You know that is still the rule, right?"

"Yes, daddy!" he laughs at my high pitch as I say his name.

"Don't let these boys fool you."

I nod and shoo him away.

"Thirty more minutes then off the phone for the night." I hear Stylus breathing into the phone. "Your Dad?" "My one and only."

"Maybe you'll say that about me soon," Stylus laughs. Daddy cranes his neck to get a view of the phone or snatch a piece of our conversation.

"Maybe," I whisper through a cupped hand over the receiver.

"What?"

"Maybe!" Daddy shakes his head and walks back downstairs.

My first day of school I feel a similar twinge of queasiness like the first day of band camp. I was jittery because I wondered if Stylus would still want to be around me. Drea tried her best to calm me down. "That boy likes you, girl," she said as she worked on my hair. "I've known Stylus for what seems like forever and the way that boy looks at you is the way he'd look at his music stand." I giggle.

"I mean, look at you. You are skinny and black like the stand so – " I stomp Drea in the foot. She winces and bops me on the head with the comb.

"Keep playing with me, hear? You'll go to school with your head half done looking like what happened!"

After getting off the bus – Daddy still held fast to the "no cars" rule – I made my way towards the band room. Stylus sat perched on the gate rail nodding hard in his headphones. I tap his leg.

"Sup sir?"

Stylus smiles and steadies his legs to open his arms for a hug.

"Bring it in, frosh. How goes it?" My head sinks into his chest. Fresh laundry and CK One.

"So far, so good."

"What your schedule looking like?"

"Band and English in the morning. Math, Spanish, and Civics in the afternoon."

"What lunch you got?"

"3rd lunch." He looks hurt.

"Ouch. I got first lunch. What floor is your class?"

"Third." He lets out a grunt.

"Damn. They ain't letting you be great at all."

"What lunch you got?"

"First. Advanced Band privileges."

"Whatever, boy."

Stylus hops off the rail. "I can sneak out and see you today. We're not doing too much."

"Like a date?" I'm hopeful.

"No, like I'm eating lunch with my little homie."

Little homie stabs me in my chest. Maybe he didn't see me like that after all. "Nah, I'm good."

Stylus reaches out for another hug but I dodge his arms. He laughs.

"You know you my girl," he winks.

***

Stylus' birthday is October 20th. His mom is throwing him a party.

"Come on through," he tells me after school. "Good food and my folks will be there." I want to get him the perfect gift. I drag my mother up and down aisles in the men's department at the mall.

"Does he like Polo shirts?"

"Yeah but he has like every color, Mama."

"Maybe cologne?"

"He only wears CK One."

Mama raises her brows. "And how do you know that?"

"I've smelled it…" I pause. "He told me that's what he sprays on his shirts."

"Uh huh." Mama looks at her watch. "We have to be there in 45 minutes."

"Mama, you're not helping." I look at the clearance rack. "Maybe a wallet?" I push one of the small squares of leather to the side. "Sunglasses maybe?" Mama shrugs.

"Don't tell Daddy." He never met Stylus but was more and more fussy about him. "Don't go out there trying to fawn over no boy that don't deserve you," he said.

"I'll handle daddy," Mama says, shooing his name in the air. "Why are we in this department store? I thought you said he liked music?"

YES!

My long strides force Mom to powerwalk to the record store. I flip through the hip hop section and R&B.

"I don't know what he doesn't have," I pout.

"Get him a gift certificate."

"But doesn't that look like I didn't try?"

"Oh, sweet pea. This is so cute."

I pay for a $25 gift card. "Dress it up with a very nice card," Mom laughs. I buy a Mahogany Hallmark card with a man on the front in a blue suit playing a saxophone under a streetlight.

Stylus lived in St. John's subdivision. Even though it was only us in the car, Mama whispered, "white folks used to live here before they moved out to the county." Before I moved my finger from the doorbell, a tall coffee colored woman answers the door. She smiles and takes my hands. "Hello! You two are the first to arrive. Stylus is in the living room watching T.V."

"Thank you, Mrs. Majors." Stylus' mother wrinkles her nose and forces a quick spurt of air out of her nose.

"No husband here. Majors is my maiden name." Pricks of panic skip across my face.

"I'm sorry, ma'am."

Ms. Majors laugh. "Girl! 'Ma'am' is as bad as Mrs." She looks past me at my mother. "You trained this one right." They laugh and slap hands. "That's the truth, honey!" Mama laughs. Ms. Majors points in Stylus' direction. "Gone in there, sugar. I'm taking your Mama out on the deck for a drink."

"Make sure it's strong," Mama jokes.

"Like us and how we trying to raise these kids to be," Ms. Majors grins. They continue to hold hands like old friends.

Stylus is spread across the couch, flipping through channels. I hit his leg with the card and gift certificate.

"Happy birthday, lil buddy."

"You just not gonna let that go, huh?"

"Nope." He sits on the couch next to me and grabs my hand.

"Can I call you my boyfriend?" I blurt out. I practiced bringing this up in the mirror all week. I wanted my voice to be smooth and raspy like Erykah Badu. Stylus said he liked the sound of her voice. Instead, I squeaked and rushed the question. Stylus laughs.

"What do you want to call me?"

I can't look him in the eye. He turns off the television and switches on the stereo.

"Do you love music?" he leans against the back of the couch and waits for my answer.

"I like it a lot." Stylus drops my hand and frowns.

"But do you love it?"

"Not like you love it." Glasses clink and our mothers' conversation drifts in from the open window. "Girl yes! With some heels…"

"Then I'm not your boyfriend." I turn and face Stylus all the way.

"That's not fair! How do I love something that you love as much as yourself? Can't I learn to love music like – "

"I love you."

I plunge my free hand deep between my thighs. The back of my head hurts from smiling so hard. I throw my arms around his neck. "But you're right." Stylus pulls me up from the sofa while I still cling to his neck. Our mothers continue laughing at something on the back porch.

He opens a door in the kitchen that leads downstairs and flips a switch.

All four of the walls are lined with vinyl records. There is a framed album cover of a man in a purple suit and white ruffled shirt sitting on a parked motorcycle on a dark street. A woman looks at him from a lit open doorway. "Who is Prince?"

"The God," Stylus sighs. I read the names on the front covers that catch my attention.

"Earth, Wind, and Fire."

"The Elements."

Dorothy Norwood. Shirley Caesar. Rick James. The Temptations. Sylvester. Freddie Jackson. Howlin' Wolf. Billie Holiday. B.B. King. The O'Jays. Brick. Cameo. Chaka Khan. Kraftwerk. We stop in front of *Innervisions*.

"This is the Apothecary."

"Why do you call down here the Apothecary?"

"My mom calls it that. She's got a record for every mood." The smell of aging paper stuffs my nose. I'm under Stylus' spell. "All of these are your mom's records?"

"Most of them are. But the older ones belonged to my Granddaddy. I remember sitting on his lap and just melting into the melodies." Stylus flips through a box of records on the floor. "Grandaddy taught me to appreciate music as a breathing and complicated thing. You know?"

I don't. But I swear to love music as hard as I love Stylus.

In the back corner there is a small collection of records displayed on a corner desk. Stylus thumps his chest. "My own collection. Updating the Apothecary a bit."

Midnight Marauders. The Diary. ATLiens. Soul Food. Supa Dupa Fly.

"Why not just buy the CDs?" Stylus sucks his teeth.

"Girl, stop. Vinyl sounds like velvet. It melts into your ear." He rubs his ear lobes. "You can hear the work. The snaps and pops. They have their own message. Sometimes you need to hear the static."

"I see." He reaches for a pair of headphones and puts them on my head.

"No, lady. Hear."

Stylus puts on a record.

"Hear it. Use your ears."

I close my eyes and focus on the acoustic guitar and the voice sighing and saying what sounds like a tiny prayer in the background. Aside from the pops and slight shaking sounds and drum drops I smile at the heavy drawl of "no ma'am" and "shawty." I squeeze Stylus' hand. He smiles and mouths the lyrics.

The ceiling shakes as someone walks through the kitchen. Ms. Majors hollers from the top of the stairs.

"Stylus! Your other company is here!"

He doesn't stop nodding and mouthing the words.

"Stylus!"

"Coming!"

He twirls me around and takes off my headphones. More steps pound across the ceiling. Ms. Majors yells down one more time.

"And boy, you better put all my albums back where you found them!"

Stylus winks and grabs my hand to walk upstairs. His love is like a song I don't want to end.

· 1 1 ·

MOVING FURNITURE

Miss Ann lived in the same tin roof house for almost an entire century. Its peeling paint and faded green shutters are unassuming. It took her daddy and granddaddy thirty years to build the house before and after work as sharecroppers in the field up the road from the house. Miss Ann liked to sit on her porch and rock, telling anybody – from lost travelers to the shut-in ministry from her church – about how her Daddy chucked wood from the bunch of pine trees behind the house to build it.

"This a borrowhouse," Miss Ann said between each creaky rock of her chair. "My daddy borrowed this and that to make it stand. Scrapped tin for the roof and a pot and split the wood between kindling and making floorboards." Miss Ann's contribution to the house was the white room, a small room with white walls and white carpet at the back of the house. Her first and only husband, Albert, built it for her as an anniversary gift. He died from pneumonia a few years later but Miss Ann made sure to take good care of the room.

The white room held her prettiest and most cherished things: a small white teacup, a white sitting couch, and a white rocking chair. Nobody was ever allowed in the white room, even without shoes.

"Gotta keep it nice," Miss Ann fussed. "I want to keep my things nice." Once a year, Miss Ann let the nice man from next door, Mr. Rufus, come and paint the walls back white. The white room was the only part of the house that didn't fade.

Every summer, Miss Ann's family came to stay at the house and catch up on the year. Girl Junior, a family nickname for Miss Ann's oldest girl, Annie, gathered the family together. It was becoming increasingly difficult to line folks' schedules up to an agreeable time. Girl Junior found herself begging longer and harder each year for her kinfolk to come and gather at Miss Ann's house.

"Please, Cousin Black. She ain't getting no younger. Naw, she doesn't have internet this year either." Girl Junior twists the bottom of her shirt and mouths obscenities to her ceiling. "I understand that you need to be near a plug. But do your favorite cousin this favor one more time. Mama only sees us once a year. Uh-huh. Of course there will be chicken! You know I still know how to flour a bird." Girl Junior laughs out loud. "Great. Thank you so much. See you soon." Girl Junior presses "end" on her cell phone. These kids were getting older and thinking themselves too busy to share any of their time with family. Girl Junior knew she would have at least ten more conversations like this one. "Who knew you'd have to beg to see family?" she asks her empty kitchen. Girl Junior picks up the phone and starts dialing the next number.

***

Shiny new impalas, dented bumper Lexuses, and thumping trucks shake Miss Ann's house. She hobbles to the rickety porch, her hand laid across the top of her face to shield the sun and look out into the road. Older folks got out of the cars in sections: feet, knees, arms and torsos. The younger folks hopped out the car in one fell swoop, slamming their car doors. Miss Ann claps her hands and smiles wide. "All that racket, I heard ya'll coming a mile down the road," she laughs as she steadies herself on the balled fist in her back.

"Hey Maw Maw," they chorused, a line of box braids and dreadlocks, low cut fades and relaxed hair, afro puffs and bald heads standing in procession to hug her neck and kiss her cheek. "What you got to eat?"

Miss Ann laughs again. "It's in there. Took me all day to cook." *I love when my babies are home.* Everybody younger than Miss Ann was one of her babies. But everyone knew to stay out the white room or risk being popped. The house floors grunt a greeting to Miss Ann's guests. Girl Junior squeezes her mother's shoulders and helps her to favorite rocking chair in the living room. The younger children gather at her feet to talk her ear off.

"Maw Maw, why don't you get a new house with Wi-Fi?" the second to oldest boy nicknamed Squeak asks.

"Why fire what now?" Miss Ann drawls in her accent.

"Why-FIE, Maw Maw." Squeak cups his mouth to make him sound louder. "The Internet."

"Don't need it."

"You BARELY got colored television with five channels," the family's baby girl Alexis, squeals. "I NEED Doc McStuffins and cartoons, Maw Maw!"

Miss Ann grins and pokes her pinky into the girl's soft tummy. Alexis still has her baby fat and giggles when Miss Ann pokes her. Alexis' brother, Anno, talks into his hand, "she's like the dough boy on TV." A cousin, Bun, snorts at Anno's joke. Miss Ann doesn't seem to hear him.

"I'ma stuff YOU, gal, and put you in my white room. With your pretty self." Alexis' eyes sparkle and her chubby cheeks bounce in rhythm with her beaded plats. "Maw Maw, why you stay out here in this ole house with nothin' and nobody nearby?"

"This here house is a keep sake. It's like museum of my life."

"More like a crypt," the oldest boy cousin, Trim, mumbles. Miss Ann pops him on the side of his head. "Don't talk bout your heritage like that boy. You chirren. So disrespectful." Miss Ann works herself up and reaches out to pop Trim again. He moves his head and stomps out the door. "Don't worry bout him Maw Maw," Anno says. "He mad because his phone ain't got no bars and the girl he likes is supposed to text him today." The other children laugh.

Miss Ann's screen door slams more than usual with people going in and out.

"You in or you out!" Girl Junior yells from the living room. "Ya'll are letting flies in!" At dusk, flecks of bright green light and hover and dance around the porch. The children beg for empty mason jars or use their bare hands to hunt lightning bugs.

"Their butts are lit up!" Alexis chirps. Alexis' mother, Dana, fusses at her daughter about saying the word "butt." "Young ladies don't say 'butt,'" she says.

Alexis puckers her mouth and thinks for a minute on her mother's warning. The word was too much fun not to say out loud again. "Butt!"

After the lightning bugs are collected and the Mason jars' glow like mini moons on the porch Miss Ann rocks the chair on the porch to thrust her forward. She starts to fumble around with the Mason jars by clicking them together and dragging a chair across the porch back into the house.

"Uh oh. She's moving furniture," Girl Junior says. "She tired of us now. It's time to go." Miss Ann's kinfolks laugh and start collecting aluminum covered plates, children, and unopened cans of soda and head to their cars. Car doors slam one more time. The jars full of lightning bugs seem to wave goodbye. After unscrewing the jars and letting the lightning bugs free – "it's just cruel to leave them in there," she said – Girl Junior sits on the porch next to Miss Ann. Cicadas sing high and loud. Girl Junior touches her hand.

"Mama, I know you hate talking about this but I don't like you out here by yourself." She pats Miss Ann's hand. "Don't you wanna move into the city limits with me?" "All that noise in the city. I like my quiet when I want it. My TV and white room keep me company."

"What about your friends? Do they still come around? Where's Miss Ira?"

Miss Ira was Miss Ann's best friend and card partner. Mama said they sat together in the same pew in church every Sunday. Miss Ira always wore her hair in a bun but folks said her hair was down her back. Her jiggly laugh made her thighs dance.

"Ira passed earlier this month in her sleep."

"Mama!" Girl Junior lays her hand on her chest. "Why didn't you say anything?"

"People die, child. That shouldn't be breaking news."

Girl Junior slaps her leg. The mosquitoes were coming out. "And Mr. Rufus? He didn't come by and say hey like he usually does?"

"He be around."

Girl Junior stands up to grab her keys and head home.

"We'll be back in the morning, Mama. Love you."

"I ain't cooking no breakfast. Ya'll eating whatever's left in the icebox. Love you back."

The next morning, the house again fills with people and Girl Junior pulls Miss Ann to her room to talk more about moving her out of the house.

"Mama, I'm serious. Come live with me. I worry bout you, out here by yourself."

"Daughter, I done told you last night I'm fine with my TV and my white room."

Girl Junior sighs and pulls a strand of her hair.

"Your white room is just things, Mama. Things. Furniture."

"Look here, girl child. I know little in this life. But my house and furniture be some of what I know." Miss Ann frowns and looks into the white room.

"I come in here and move the furniture around and talk to it so that it doesn't become restless."

"Restless? Talk to it? Mama…" Girl Junior shakes her head. She fears her mother losing her wits about her and living alone. Girl Junior makes a mental note to call her Mama's doctor on Monday for an appointment. "You're coming back with me tonight. That does it." Miss Ann raises her eyebrows. Girl Junior softens her voice. "I'm worried bout you, Mama. That's all. You're coming home with me tonight and that's final."

Something in the white room creaks.

"Must be time to move the furniture," Miss Ann grunts. "They ain't just things, Girl Junior. They special."

"Why?" Girl Junior grew up around all of the things in the white room. As a girl, dusting the house was her job on Saturday mornings. She dusted every corner and wiped down every surface in the house except the white room. Miss Ann took care of the white room on her own. The only time Girl Junior remembered being allowed into the white room was for a picture for prom and her first wedding. Miss Ann said didn't think it was necessary to have a second wedding photo in the room.

"Used to be people," she says.

"Owned by people?"

"No. *Pee-pole*." Miss Ann exaggerates her last word and stomps her foot. Girl Junior sighs and sucks her teeth.

"Mama, where's your mind at right now?"

Miss Ann stands up straight and defiant. "Don't sass me, girl. Don't forget who you are talking to now."

For the first time in her life Girl Junior sits on the small couch in the room. Miss Ann clicks her teeth and stares. The couch wriggles. Girl Junior jumps up and hollers.

"That couch you just sat on frighten you? It didn't bite you, did it?" Miss Ann laughs. "Farmer ain't mean you no harm."

"Farmer? Is the name of the company who made the couch?"

"Naw," Miss Ann shakes her head. "Farmer was the name of the census man who came to the house causing mischief in 1920. He was rude and just assumed he knew about black folks. Assumed the house wasn't ours. Assumed I weren't married – " Miss Ann pauses and waves her had in the air. "I mean, I weren't married at that time but he ain't know that." The couch continues to wiggle and moves slightly to the left. Girl Junior sidesteps behind her mother. "How you doing that Mama?" she shrieks. Miss Ann is unbothered. "I told you gal that is a census man. Reckon he happy to see somebody else other than my old and wrinkly face." Miss Ann stoops over to push the small couch over to the left. Girl Junior never noticed the scrapes in the floor. She's afraid to ask if they were fingernail marks or scratches left from her Mama moving the furniture around. Miss Ann leans against the couch. "He didn't believe Coloreds could own a house. He just barged in and jotted in his notebook and shook his head. I made sure he didn't get back up off it. Since he knew black folk so well I made sure he became part of us and part of the house."

Girl Junior gasped. "*How* Mama?"

Miss Ann shrugs. "I know a little of this and that. Don't worry yourself bout it." Miss Ann pulls herself up and motions to Girl Junior to follow her. The laughter and talking in the front of the house seems more and more distant.

"Come on in here all the way. Might as well tell you some truths."

Girl Junior takes small and fragile steps into the room. Miss Ann points at the tiny porcelain teacup with pink and gold flowers.

"Pretty little thing ain't it?" Miss Ann fingers the rim of the cup. She kisses the handle. "I was carrying you when a lil ole gal bammed on my door one night during a thunderstorm begging to come in and hide from her man that was beating on her." Miss Ann looks past Girl Junior and into a different time. "She slapped him across the face with a skillet full of frying meat. She was a small thing, couldn't of been older than eighteen or twenty. She was scared to death cause her man was white and pretty well known around these parts – " Miss Ann whispers – "as somebody with a wife." Girl Junior tries to hold her mouth closed. "I told that gal she can stay here for safety. There she is. Safe."

Girl Junior stares at her mother, the old woman with a quick laugh and slumping shoulders. Miss Ann moves toward her rocking chair, careful to sit all of her achy bones in the seat, and rocks.

"Your white room is a museum of folks that you want to remember?"

"That's right."

Girl Junior takes a deep breath and sighs her final question.

"So who is your rocking chair?"

"Mr. Rufus."

· 1 2 ·

SOME KIND OF WONDERFUL
Illustrated by John Jennings and Stacey Robinson

Figure 12.1: The Hurricane

I haven't seen sunshine in 2005 days, not since the calm of the last storm. No, not that one. You'd think folks would've learned and put a plan in place. But they treated this storm like Katrina, with hopes and prayers of ancestral protection and government know-how. Nope. This storm danced a similar path out into the middle of the gulf but was fickle and didn't want to be outdone by *her* ancestor Katrina. She decided to swing back around to the coast and claw her way to the middle of each southern state. Katrina told her where to scream, where to push, and where to bend us. As the Dixie winds whistled outside our door, I asked my Daddy about whether or not we should move north.

"We ain't near enough to the coast to worry," Daddy said. I believed him. He spoke with bass in his voice deep enough for me to believe everything he said was a fact.

I remember the storm's wailing the most. I couldn't tell if it was the wind or Miss Sandra and Miss Livvy, our next door neighbors who invited me over for peach cobbler with extra thick crust on holidays, pushing their weight against the door to keep it shut. Daddy leaned his weight up against the door too, along with his favorite chair and his work bench.

"Stay in the middle!" he yelled. This Hurricane Bitch walked each street in Crescent, Mississippi. She called to us with thunder. Trees bent and snapped underneath her angry walk. Winds sashayed her way up Sip Street, running her hand through the open stalls at the farmer's market and turning over tables and orphaned fruit and vegetables. She kept on walking, stomping down Honky-tonk Alley and getting drunk on the moonshine liquor behind the counter of the Cake Factory, the juke joint and local brothel. When she was good and drunk, Hurricane Bitch settled in the middle of the town and sang her own Blues. Upset that no one came out to woo or comfort her, she yelled and stumbled towards the Crescent River and kicked with all her might. The water swell hid her tears. My whole neighborhood washed away with one large crack of lightning and a tumble of water. Water sucked at our house, leaving Daddy's with a pulsing vein on the side of his forehead. The water sucked at us like a mosquito, pulling us down, way down into moving darkness. I moved from the middle to the side of Daddy's bobbing body and out the door.

Hurricane Bitch came to destroy.

***

I woke up in the most southern part of Mississippi. I tried clearing my head but electric blue and toxic green floodlights blinded me. A rickety metal sign turned on its side said "Welcome to New Jackson." Someone crossed out New Jackson and spray painted "The Soup." I would find out later why it was called the Soup: Hurricane Bitch completely blew out the thin dam that separated the clean water from the hydrocution water. Hydrocution powered the city. It was a substitute for the death penalty in order to find alternative sources of energy. Peoples' bodies were drained of their fluids and it was converted to a low level supply of power. Leftover bodies sometimes floated into the drinking water.

The only thing that saved the Soup from falling into the Gulf after the storms was their platforms. The platforms were damaged; they dipped and slid into the ground until they become lopsided. The Soup split into three zones: Limbo, the Bottoms, and the Trap. Limbo is at the top. It is the least affected by the storm and recognizable by a lone crumbling skyscraper where most of the residents live. Limbo was the last ditch effort to show money: the tower's gate showcased barbed wire and red flags in the front and back. They believed all the wrong of the world would get caught on the wire and out of their sight. They never ventured out past Revenant Boulevard, the main street. Limboers were people who could still afford to put on airs. They clung to the hope that their jacks could save them. Jacks are electric money and kept on cards and chips in folks' hands. Limboers never went past the barbwire gate. They found hydrocution useful in keeping down crime and keeping up their airs with readily available electricity. They were not zone minglers and did not socialize past the gate. Limboers socialized via foils or hologram versions of themselves into each others' cyberspaces.

The Bottoms was a mix of people down on their luck and unable to scrap together enough jacks to get a room in the higher zone. They reminded me most of Crescent, with bunched shotgun houses, loud rickety steps, and even louder rickety laughter. One Bottoms dweller, Mr. Flint, told me told me most Bottoms dwellers didn't want to deal with the bullshit of being in Limbo. I stayed in a small room on DeMarritt Avenue with a view of the silhouette of the hydrocution plant.

The Trap is the last tier of the Soup. It sits at the base of the city's floodlights. Trap potholes are big enough for kids to play hide and seek or wind up missing. Empty slouch pouches – GMO food slop – scurry down the streets. The trap was closest to the hydrocution sludge. Mutated bodies –the folk – stumbled around the streets with slipping and cracked skin.

Figure 12.2: The folk

The folk were the unfortunate souls who lost the most during the storm. Without sanctuary, they were exposed to the elements and to the waste of the hydrocution plants. They mutated quickly: extra limbs, excess hanging skin, and cocked third eyes grew from their bodies. The folk rarely ventured out of the trap. They feared being arrested for simply being alive and then hydrocuted. The Trap was the place where fucks didn't grow.

***

In the streets they call it Hack. It is a drug that got its start as a computer program started by the Environmental Protection Agency to clean the quickly dwindling water supply in Limbo. Nanobots – nicknamed bugs – were supposed to be less evasive than harsh bleaching and stripping. They sought out and ate the material and inorganic waste foreign to the environment. One of the waste workers who deposited and disposed of used bugs accidentally inhaled them after taking off his mask. The bugs moved through his system and he got hot and happy. The guy supposedly grabbed a vial full of bugs and shared them with a buddy who was a computer coder. They learned the bot codes and tried to replicate them to sell but the code turned into a virus and changed the user's brain chemistry until they hallucinated and became addicted to the effect. The bugs build up under the users' skin and burn their way out. The virus was autodidactic, seeking out new users on the dark web.

How Hackers consume the drug indicates where they live in the Soup. Hack comes in gigs or bytes. Limboers used Mindreader, a form of Hack where the bugs are inhaled and result in a quick shot to the brain. Mindreader is the purest source of Hack and hardest to come by in the Soup. A gig of Mindreader was at least 1500 jacks. Limboers could afford to buy Hack by the gigs. Bottoms dwellers and the folk hacked by the byte. Hack in the Bottoms and trap was nicknamed "Dirty Syringes." The coding in these bugs meant they had to be injected under the skin. Dirty Syringes was junk code and often recycled bugs. The bugs eat through the veins before reaching the brain and releasing and endorphins.

Hack wasn't regulated in the Trap. It led to desperate folk doing criminal acts for a chance at a hit. Crime is what kept the plant fed and the Soup functioning. Part of those desperate acts were the Trap Games. When the Trap games first started it was daring young Limboers – they called themselves Norms – venturing to the Trap to see if they could find a cheap thrill. When they realized – and probably smelled – the desperation of the folk, they used folk begging for jacks to get a cheap thrill. Norms started out with annoying dares to get a rise out of the folk for their amusement:

"Slap the shit out of that other thing over there and I'll give you ten jacks."

Pulled by a hunger deeper than embarrassment, the folk would slap each other. As the demand for Hack grew, the taunts became more lethal and grimy. Slaps turned to slap boxing. Slap boxing turned to full out brawls. Brawls turned into private and corporatized events.

After going corporate the Trap Games took place at the Hippodrome. It was a burnt out factory with two main floors and broken windows. The walls were still charred on the first level, the threshing floor. Only folk fought on this level and it was a fight to sudden death. The loser was dragged to their death and hydrocuted. The roar of the crowd was not as loud as the trap music, a heavy droning of bass and synthesizers. The sheer loudness of the music and the deafening crowd added to the frenzy of the folk thrashing each other for entertainment. After sudden death was a brief pause of silence and the winner climbed six flights of stairs – the stairway to heaven – to face their next opponent.

Figure 12.3: Heli recruiting Blanka for the Trap Games

The elevator was reserved for Norms. The top level of the Hippodrome was the penthouse. Cream colored sofas and a chandelier sparkled in the flood-light. The bass from the music downstairs vibrated through the floor. A marble fireplace sat at the back of the room. The windows were stainglass to hide the ugliness of the outside world. Attendees wore black tuxedos and sequined gowns and were waited on by disfigured hands in white gloves underneath silver plates full of champagne, fresh fruit, and caviar. The penthouse fights were often folks versus norms. Norms paid a flat fee (usually a j-note or 2000 jacks) to fight the winner from the Threshing Floor. Folk were told during their climb up the stairs whether or not they were fighting a norm. They were told to go easy on their opponent in exchange for their life, extra Hack, or a good meal after the fight.

I fought in my first bout three nights after I arrived in the Soup. I looked rough and hadn't slept in days. My appearance must've caught the attention of Heli, a scout for the Trap Games.

"Are you from the Trap?" he asked.

"The what?"

"The trap. That shithole closest to the muck." He spits between a wide gap in his teeth.

"I ain't from here."

"Where you from?"

"None of your damn business."

Heli laughs and walks around me.

"Nope. Definitely not a folk."

"A what?"

"Shutup. Let me look at you."

He continues to slowly circle around me and extends an index finger to poke me. I grab it and turn it backwards. He hollers and slaps me to the ground and laughs between groans of pain.

"Yeah," he huffs grabbing his broken finger. "You are just what we need in the Trap Games."

A piece of my unkept hair shivers in my face.

"What do I need to do for the Trap Games?"

"Survive."

I fought the next night. My opponent was a folk. She was slouchy and her skin was gangrene. Her pupils bled to either side of her eye. The girl folk lunged at me with three hands and foam on her mouth. She was easy enough to fend off, hoping her appearance would throw me off. Ole girl knocked me down and I found a rusted pipe. I swung it upside her head and she fell instantly.

Figure 12.4: Blanka versus the folk

"SUDDEN DEATH" a voice shouts from the speaker.

A pair of metal arms whirs to live and picks up the girl's body. She screamed as she was dragged towards a hydrocution pipe with "ASYLUM" spray-painted in red blocked graffiti letters. The roar of the crowd drowned out any thought of remorse or emotion.

I climbed the Stairway to Heaven hoping to regain a sense of myself. The smell of frying fish and alcohol takes me to someplace in my head that's familiar. But the wonderful smell of real food clashed with the stench of my own sweat and blood of the loser girl folk. I arrive to the disappointed looks of Norms. They don't want to see me fight one of their own. "Looks like you live to fight another day, trap star," a man with a curly mustache says to me. "Go ahead and eat and drink over in that corner."

I stumbled out of the Hippodrome drunk on gin and a stomach full of fried fish and caviar. I heard someone call down to me from the penthouse.

"Blanka!"

It was Heli. He was waving a bandaged hand to tell me to hold up and wait for him. I nod but make sure I have enough room to run.

"You left before I got to give you this." A silver vial sat in the middle of his palm.

Figure 12.5: Sudden death

"Your payment for the night."

"I already ate."

"Okay. Well, consider this a bonus."

His hand is still outstretched. I stare at the vial.

"You a country bitch ain't you? Where you from again?"

"I'm from Crescent." I spit at his feet. "What is it?"

"Something that will change your life," he said. I roll my eyes. There was always some new shit or some new high or somebody claiming they had life changing something or another.

"Ever heard of Hack?"

"I heard some people talking about bugs. Is that the same thing?"

"A version of it. This is the pure shit."

"Pure?"

"You pop the top and inhale." Heli brings the closed vial up to his nose and smiles.

"I'ma stick with weed."

"That's yesterday, Blank."

"So?"

"This is like weed with a brain!" I look him in his face. His left eyelid twitches like it was thinking.

"That don't make any sense."

Heli's fat cheeks wobble.

"I hurt your feelings?"

"Naw. No hurt feelings over here. Just trying to bring you into THIS fucking century."

"Uh huh."

He rolls the small vial between his grubby index finger and thumb. Heli clicks his front teeth.

"They call this Professor. It's the top of the line Mindreader Hack. It learns what you like and teaches you a lil' something."

"Clever." Heli laughs.

"Makes you feel like a fucking genius! Best two j-notes of your life."

"I don't have that kind of money."

Heli shrugs and pushes the vial into my hand.

"Consider this an advance for your next bouts."

My palm burns and itches. I hear small pops from the tiny bots.

"Oh they ready," Heli laughs.

"Teach me something, professor."

I close my eyes and close my left nostril and inhale.

Swirls of yellow and orange heat brush my face. Goosebumps cover my arms and neck. Every hair I have stands on edge and tiny feet march across my scalp and behind my ears. I feel my eyes glaze over and when I blink to clear the tears I see Crescent. Miss Sandra and Miss Livvy are arguing and snapping peas. Daddy's stereo is blasting his favorite Blues record. He's sitting on the porch, shaking his head and laughing at Sandra and Livvy. I smell honeysuckle. Daddy starts to laugh. An itch creeps through the deepest part of my brain. I start to hit the side of my head. Each slap Daddy's mouth grows and his laugh becomes louder and insane. The itch crawls into my eyelids and I rub my eyes. After a hard blink I'm staring into Heli's face. "Ugh."

Figure 12.6: Teach me something, professor

"How was that?"

"Painful."

"What? You didn't get a sense of being happy?"

"It was a lie."

"You think too damn much. Maybe another hit." Heli digs into pockets.

"Maybe not. How much do those vials go for in the Trap?"

"In the Trap?" Heli rolls his eyes. "Didn't I tell you this was top of the line shit? We got out of the Soup to get this product."

"I want in."

Heli raises his eyebrows in amusement.

"You win one fight and think you can run the Trap huh?"

"I know it."

I was a trap star and stayed in the penthouse. The Trap Games were my hustle. Part of myself was lost in the sludge after that first night. I picked up a hunger. Not for food – I was fed very well – but for the hustle. Heli slipped me new Hack after each win as long as I cut him in on my profits. I didn't waste my time with the folk. I moved past jacks fairly quickly. I worked in the Bottoms and in the penthouse. Especially what we nicknamed "Penthouse after dark." J-Notes, sex, and liquor flowed freely. People wanted to extend their good time. I helped them do it with an endless supply of Mindreader. When everyone was in a stupor, I slipped out and headed to the Bottoms.

***

I'll never forget my last opponent Goodi. She could pass for a Norm. Long purple and gold hair. Hazel eyes with bright green flecks. No visible missing limbs or empty sockets. Her lashes fluttered with a slight head movement and saddened her otherwise steely gaze. She was fine. I don't know what she was fighting for. All I know was that I was in her way. And she wasn't having that shit.

The announcer held on to her name like a music note over the droning stereos.

"Goooooodiiiiiiiiiiiiiiiiiiiii!" She quickly shoots a hand up in acknowledgement of the crowd but never looks at me. Goodi keeps her head down and focuses on the floor and the music. She nods her head angrily. The MLG airhorn sounds and Goodi doesn't move. She rolls her eyes.

"Goodi...Goodi...Goodi..."

She casually turns her back to me and shrugs. I think this is my chance to make a move and attack. I shake my head to clear it and run towards her turned back. She doesn't flinch. Suddenly she turns around and here eyes are glowing green. Her stare throws me off balance and the floor dips upward. I can't move. Her face is twisted and angry and her mouth full of jagged teeth.

"What the hell are you?" I yell. But the crowd drowns out my voice to just a lip synch.

"Your death dealer," she sneers. As long as I stare into her eyes I'm paralyzed. I force myself to think, to break free of Goodi's mindfuck. I think about Crescent and my Daddy. *I am powerful.*

Goodi reaches for my throat. I knee her to get free. My knee in her groin surprises her and her glowing eyes die down back to hazel. Goodi was vulnerable and I was ready. I grab both sides of her head and head butt her into submission. Goodi screams and falls on her back. ASYLUM springs to life. It's hungry.

The speakers beat like erratic hearts. Almost time. I smash Goodi's head into the dirt and wait for her to stop squirming. The song changes.

"Here we go...climbing the stairway to heaven..."

I push her face deeper into the floor. Goodi stops moving. An electric whirring comes from the corner of the threshing floor. Metal arms snake towards Goodi's body, ready to claim its prize. I roll out of the way. I think we're done. A hand grabs my leg. She's not dying alone.

The arms sink into our bodies like teeth, dragging us with eager welcome towards ASYLUM.

DISCUSSION QUESTION BANK

"A Visitation from Grace"

1. What is the significance of voice in the story? For example, compare and contrast Mayfield's voluntary muteness with the speakerbox. How are they similar? Different?
2. Discuss the phrase "chose is chose." What does it mean?
3. The Blackshear townspeople gathered together for "the benediction," an effort to help the family of the chosen grieve the loss of their loved one. What is the significance of the community in the grieving process? Do you think the townspeople are healing from the losses the community continues to suffer?
4. Discuss the following quote: "Her body wanted to pass the fight on to someone with younger bone marrow and redder blood, but in the quietest corner of Grace's spirit she knew she still had work to do." How does this build upon the idea of older generations' lack of belief in younger people's work for freedom?
5. Write an alternative ending for what happens to Mayfield. Where does he go?

"Intentions"

1. Present an argument for whether or not Picklebean is an anti-hero.
2. How does Picklebean de-romanticize the efforts of the Civil Rights Movement? Use passages from the story to help support your ideas.
3. Discuss the symbolism of Picklebean's suit. What does it represent? Why?
4. Why is it important to remember the people who worked behind-the-scenes when discussing the Civil Rights Movement? What additional layers do their stories add to the historical narrative in place?
5. Describe the type of project you would submit for Dream Week. What would it include? Why?

"Between the Hedges"

1. How does the story build upon the idea of black exceptionalism as a requirement for success? How is this idea passed down generation-to-generation?
2. Discuss Art Senior's hesitation to let Pap/Junior try out for the white football team. What lesson was Art Senior trying to teach him?
3. What lesson(s) do you think Pap wanted to teach Reese with his college story? Do they overlap with the lessons that his father, Art Senior, tried to teach him? Use examples from the story to help support your ideas.
4. Although "Between the Hedges" is based on the University of Georgia, other predominantly white colleges were also confronted with issues of segregation in the American South. Discuss Pap's response to Reese's acceptance into UGA. How does it symbolize the challenges of integration and segregation in southern schools?
5. Do you think Pap/Junior showed cowardice or courage by walking away from football tryouts? Why or why not?

"Good Bleach"

1. Compare and contrast the act of remembering by Auntie Nan and by the man in the hospital room next door. How do they remember love?
2. What do you think are the "black specks" Auntie Nan talks about when she was cleaning the eighth floor of the hospital?
3. How does the story use the theme of cleanliness to develop its plot and characters? Use examples from the story to help illustrate your ideas.

4. Compare and contrast how Uncle Joe shows love to Percy and Auntie Nan. How does it help heal and encourage them similarly? Differently?
5. After reading the story, how do you define good bleach?

"Beautiful Ones"

1. Sister uses social media to get the word out about her missing brother. How does this move our understanding of protest in the South away from the traditional Civil Rights Movement narrative?
2. The reader is provided multiple accounts of Stinney's personality and life. Discuss the significance of differing views about Stinney's character. How do these perspectives influences whether or not it is safe for the reader to be sympathetic towards him?
3. Compare and contrast how Stinney and Sister's mother approaches them differently about being respectable and successful in life. What are the similarities and differences?
4. Discuss the exchange between Sister's Mama and Mr. McGillis. Do you think he was genuinely interested in "telling the truth" about Stinney or looking for a sensational story? Use examples from the story to anchor your ideas.
5. How can we read this story as a coming-of-age narrative for Sister?

"Happy Feelins"

1. Discuss how the story highlights the difficulty of being a family member of someone who is incarcerated. For example, how does the story tackle issues of fatherhood and love? Use examples from the story to anchor your ideas.
2. What does the white prison light symbolize in the story? How can we use this imagery to think about Radiant's character?
3. How does the story complicate ideas of happiness? Use passages from the story to support your discussion points.
4. Discuss the attitude of Bezzle's grandfather in the story. What does it symbolize? How does his approach to protecting Bezzle compare to Bezzle's mother or father?
5. How does Radiant symbolizes the prison industrial complex and black men?

"Splish-Splash"

1. The story presents the reader with an arch of racism: from subtle to very direct and violent actions against black people in the past and present. How are these actions reflective of the complex and non-linear race relations in the contemporary American South?
2. Compare and contrast Jefferson Street Pool and Radium Springs pool. What do they symbolize? Pay particular attention to the importance of how water is held and described.
3. Discuss the significance of Mr. Shill checking the dirtiness of the pool water. What does he and he actions represent?
4. Write a second stanza to the children's work song. What would it say? Why?
5. Discuss Phoebe's incident. How did it make you feel? What does her treatment by the police officer suggest about the treatment of black women and girls in general?

"Skin Carnival"

1. Discuss the title of the story. What does it mean? How does it give insight into the plot of the story?
2. Create a character profile for Yam. What are his strengths? Weaknesses? How does he grow more confident in himself at the end of the story?
3. Discuss the symbolism of the fair's "Hell House" and Yam's exploration of his sexuality. What does the Hell House represent? Why is it significant that it is the background for Yam's self-discovery?
4. Share your thoughts about what you think Yam means when he says he doesn't want to be saved. Is he talking about religion or something else? Use examples from the stories to support your argument.
5. Discuss how life and death are symbolized in the story. How do they help develop the story? Use passages from the story to help anchor your ideas.

"As Above So Below"

1. Talk about the loss or sustaining of innocence in the story. What role does Hanky and Toot's imagination play in the development of the story?
2. Why does Mam insist on buying a house in front of a "white folks cemetery?" What is the significance of her intentions?

3. Discuss the description of the flood water. What does the rising flood water make you think about? What do you think it symbolizes?
4. Discuss the significance of faith in Mam's treatment of the flood. How does she use faith to help keep her family's spirits lifted?
5. What does the coffin symbolize at the end of the story?

"The Apothecary"

1. Create an annotated playlist (5–7 songs or albums) that would be your life's soundtrack. What artists and/or titles did you pick? Why?
2. How is the act of listening important to understanding the plot of the story? Provide examples to help anchor your ideas.
3. Stylus tells the story of how his mother and grandfather influenced his musical tastes and life. How does music help bridge together generational thoughts and ideas?
4. How does the story title apply to both music and the characterization of Stylus?
5. Discuss music's role in how we view society today. How can it be used to think about how we construct community and personal relationships?

"Moving Furniture"

1. What role does family play in the development of the story?
2. Describe Miss Ann's role as a matriarch. How does this role help the reader understand her special collection in the white room?
3. Do you think Girl Junior believes her mother? What do you think happens after she discovers the secret of the white room?
4. Discuss Miss Ann's reasoning behind the special objects in the white room. Is she justified in describing her collection as "nice things?" Use examples from the story to anchor your ideas.
5. Write a backstory for one of the enchanted objects in Miss Ann's white room. Make sure to include a detailed account of their lives before and after their encounter with Miss Ann.

"Some Kind of Wonderful"

1. What do you think the title "Some Kind of Wonderful" means? How does the story title hint at the message of the story? Use examples from the story to help illustrate your argument.

2. Discuss the significance of the illustrations accompanying the story. How does illustrating the story impact impact its message differently than other stories in the book?
3. How does the environment and environmental disaster define society in this version of a future south? Use passages from the story to support your ideas.
4. What are some of the dangers and saving graces of technology presented in the story?
5. Discuss the significance of learning about the South from the perspective of a black woman. How does Blanka's narrative challenge who can speak for the American South and how the South is conceptualized?

ROCHELLE BROCK & CYNTHIA DILLARD
Executive Editors

Black Studies and Critical Thinking is an interdisciplinary series which examines the intellectual traditions of and cultural contributions made by people of African descent throughout the world. Whether it is in literature, art, music, science, or academics, these contributions are vast and far-reaching. As we work to stretch the boundaries of knowledge and understanding of issues critical to the Black experience, this series offers a unique opportunity to study the social, economic, and political forces that have shaped the historic experience of Black America, and that continue to determine our future. Black Studies and Critical Thinking is positioned at the forefront of research on the Black experience, and is the source for dynamic, innovative, and creative exploration of the most vital issues facing African Americans. The series invites contributions from all disciplines but is specially suited for cultural studies, anthropology, history, sociology, literature, art, and music.

Subjects of interest include (but are not limited to):

- EDUCATION
- SOCIOLOGY
- HISTORY
- MEDIA/COMMUNICATION
- RELIGION/THEOLOGY
- WOMEN'S STUDIES

- POLICY STUDIES
- ADVERTISING
- AFRICAN AMERICAN STUDIES
- POLITICAL SCIENCE
- LGBT STUDIES

For additional information about this series or for the submission of manuscripts, please contact Dr. Brock (University of North Carolina at Greensboro) at r_brock@uncg.edu or Dr. Dillard (University of Georgia) at cdillard@uga.com.

To order other books in this series, please contact our Customer Service Department:

(800) 770-LANG (within the U.S.)
(212) 647-7706 (outside the U.S.)
(212) 647-7707 FAX

Or browse online by series at www.peterlang.com.